DATE DUE

The Deadly Stroke

By Warren Tute

Warren Tute

The Deadly Stroke

Introduction by John Colville

Coward, McCann & Geoghegan, Inc.

New York

First American Edition 1973

SBN: 698-10501-X

Library of Congress Catalog Card Number: 72-87579

Printed in the United States of America

For John and
Deirdre Coleman

Contents

Illustrations follow page 126

Acknowledgments

I could not have written this particular book about Mers-el-Kebir without the initial help and continuing support of my old Paris friends Lieutenant John Coleman M.B.E. R.N.V.R. *Croix de Guerre* and Bar, *Médaille de la Résistance*, and of his wife, Deirdre, to whom I have dedicated the book. They introduced me to *Vice-Amiral d'Escadre* Jean Witrand, who spent six years of his distinguished career as French Naval Attaché in London and whose understanding, experience and warm co-operation have been invaluable.

Admiral Witrand then put me in touch with the key French naval officers in this story who are still alive and the experiences of *Capitaine de Vaisseau* Bernard Dufay, *Commandants* André Libiot and Maurice Putz on board the *Dunkerque* form an integral part of the book.

Others on the French side whose ready co-operation I would like to salute are Admiral Gensoul himself who, at the age of ninety, gave me his time and all the help I needed, together with his son-in-law *Commandant le Baron* Bourgeois, *Vice-Amiral* Rosset (late of the *Strasbourg*), *Capitaine de Vaisseau* Pillet (late of the Fleet Destroyers at Mers-el-Kebir) and other French naval officers, some of them still on the active list, who, for various reasons, do not wish to be mentioned by name.

In spite of a natural wariness in official circles and of being warned off the course by the British Embassy in Paris (after considerable behind-the-scenes help from the Naval Attaché), I was astonished at the warmth of friendly co-operation I received from French naval officers and for this I tender my gratitude and appreciation.

The English survivors were equally forthcoming and helpful. Having been an Admiral's Secretary myself, I went first of all to the 'scratches' of Force H at that time and so express my thanks to Commander W. J. Farrell O.B.E. D.S.C. R.N., who was Admiral Somerville's Secretary, to my friend and contemporary Commander

John Rennie O.B.E. R.N., who was Secretary to the Chief of Staff, to Captain Jasper Parrott C.B.E. R.N., Secretary to the late Vice-Admiral Wells, and to Commander the Reverend W. R. Tinniswood A.K.C. R.N., Secretary to the late Captain C. S. Holland R.N.

Mrs Cedric Holland, too, was kind enough to give me her personal recollections of that time and to lend me her husband's contemporaneous papers which were so clear and alive that it was as if he had been talking to me himself.

To Rear-Admiral G. K. Collett C.B. D.S.C. (one time Naval Liaison Officer to the Free French Forces), to Rear-Admiral T. L. Eddison C.B. D.S.C. (Gunnery Officer of HMS *Renown* at the time of these events), to the late Rear-Admiral Sir Anthony Buzzard Bart C.B. D.S.O. O.B.E. (Staff Officer [Plans] to Force H), to Rear-Admiral Keith Campbell-Walter C.B. (Flag Lieutenant and Signal Officer to Force H at that time), to Captain G. H. Peters D.S.C. R.N. and Lieutenant Commander J. J. S. Hocker R.N., late of HMS *Foxhound*, to Commander G. H. Birley R.N. late Staff Officer (Intelligence) at Gibraltar, to Lieutenant Commanders Lionel Pugh and Geoffrey Cook M.B.E. R.N.V.R., late of Gibraltar and the Admiralty War Room respectively, I am indebted for facts and personal memories which brought those days alive to me in a unique way even after thirty years.

I am most grateful to the Musée Nationale Maritime in Paris for making available to me photographs from their large collection and permitting me to reproduce them in this book.

Finally to Major General Sir Edward Spears K.B.E. C.B. M.C., I am grateful for a warm and frank discussion and for an introduction to the late Major Sir Desmond Morton K.C.B. C.M.G., who gave me invaluable personal recollections of that time shortly before he died at the age of eighty in the late summer of 1971.

Introduction

In June, 1940, I was one of the private secretaries to the Prime Minister. The decision of the British War Cabinet to control or, if that proved impossible, neutralise the French Navy, which seemed unnecessary to the British sailors at Gibraltar and outrageous to the French sailors at Oran, was scarcely less distasteful to the members of the War Cabinet themselves and to Whitehall as a whole. However, in London it appeared logical, unavoidable and desperately urgent. Warren Tute describes the shock and dismay felt by many people throughout the world when they learned that the British had opened fire on allies with whom they had so recently been fighting side by side. In this Introduction I try to explain why the War Cabinet ordered Admiral Somerville to issue an ultimatum to the French Fleet and why, in my view, their order was justified.

The unhappy but unanimous Cabinet conclusion that the French Fleet provided so grave a threat seems strange today; but it must be judged in the wide perspective of the prospects lying before the United Kingdom at the beginning of July 1940. The decision was supported by the First Lord of the Admiralty A. V. Alexander (not himself a member of the War Cabinet), and by the First Sea Lord, Sir Dudley Pound; and it was accepted immediately after the event by de Gaulle, though he subsequently attributed to it his failure to obtain more recruits for the Free French Forces. The events at Oran were only part of a much wider operation embracing the mainly peaceful seizure of French ships lying at Portsmouth, Plymouth, Alexandria, Martinique and, eventually Dakar. Those at Algiers were out of reach.

The French Navy was the fourth largest in the world, ranking behind those of Great Britain, the United States and Japan.

With two new, if as yet not fully completed, battleships, two of the most modern battlecruisers afloat, and a series of 8″ cruisers, the addition of its strength to the fleets of Germany and Italy would have challenged the supremacy of the Royal Navy. Winston Churchill had told the House of Commons on 25th June that 'the safety of Great Britain and the British Empire is powerfully, though not decisively, affected by what happens to the French Fleet'.

Even before Dunkirk, Churchill had realised that the French Army was irremediably defeated and that neither the Generals nor their troops had the spirit to fight a new Battle of the Marne. Invasion of the British Isles was threatened. We had all but lost our army; its re-equipment would take time and its most recent battle experience had been in hurried evacuations. Fighter Command of the R.A.F. was the front and indeed the vital line of defence. However, although nobody overseas believed them, the British were still thinking in terms of winning the war, not merely of surviving until some compromise peace terms were offered. To this end naval supremacy was vital, for we were fighting on exterior lines. We should sooner or later have to transport armies abroad; and we could both feed and equip ourselves only if we had the indisputable power to import food, arms, raw materials and machinery from North America and the Asiatic and African Empire. Moreover if invasion were attempted, it would be essential to contain the German fleet in its own ports.

Admiral Darlan, unchallenged arbiter of French naval policy, had pledged that the French Fleet should never fall into German hands. It was a pledge that he doubtless intended to keep, but to sail his ships into British ports seemed to him and to others in the French Government the surest guarantee that France would not be given reasonably generous armistice terms and would be occupied by German troops in its entirety.

Neither the British Government nor indeed General de Gaulle viewed this possibility with quite the same dismay as did Pétain, Weygand and Darlan. To the British and de Gaulle what mattered was that France should continue fighting, using her Empire and in particular North Africa as the base of operations. In a last, desperate effort to keep the French Prime Minister, Paul Reynaud, in power and France in the war, the British Government even offered, on 16th June, a total union of England and France. It was a Free French proposal, conceived by Jean Monnet and René Pleven and communicated to Captain David Margesson, the Government Chief Whip, on 14th June. That evening Margesson, who had discovered that Sir Horace Wilson, Secretary to the Treasury, and Sir Robert Vansittart also favoured the idea, with some difficulty convinced Neville Chamberlain and Lord Halifax who were dining together at 11 Downing Street. Churchill was informed after dinner but brushed the scheme aside as a hare-brained fantasy. However, by Sunday, 16th June, it was clear that Reynaud's influence was being rapidly superseded by that of Pétain and Weygand, the most powerful exponents of an armistice. Although the French Government had solemnly undertaken to make no separate peace, the British War Cabinet had, much to de Gaulle's dismay, agreed to release them from their pledge, at least to the extent of inquiring what kind of armistice terms might be granted, provided, and only provided, the French Fleet were despatched to British ports. Now, it seemed, a new French Government might be tempted to seek an armistice without fulfilling this condition. Therefore Churchill, who by the morning of the 16th had forgotten the proposal for an Anglo-French Union, and was intending to entertain de Gaulle, Anthony Eden and General Dill to luncheon at Chequers, returned hastily to London, lunched with de Gaulle, who was a recent convert to the undigested scheme of Union, and in the afternoon considered a draft Declaration with the War Cabinet. Reynaud, consulted by telephone, was enthusiastic: in these circumstances, he said, the French would fight on because they would see 'the ray of light at the end of the tunnel'.

Reynaud fell before this grand design, which would have carried in its train many intractable problems, but also, per-haps, the first germ of European unity, could proceed further.

The way was clear for the defeatist majority in the French Cabinet to sue for terms. British thought thus became concentrated on saving the French Fleet, more particularly when General Noguès, the most important of the French Colonial Governors, chose, after some wavering, to remain loyal to Pétain. His decision meant that any lingering hope of France continuing the struggle from colonial bases had vanished.

The German armistice terms provided that the French ships should be demobilised under German or Italian control but, with the exception of units necessary for coast surveillance and mine sweeping (an exception which could have been liberally interpreted by the Germans), should not be actively employed in the war. This, in British eyes, was a derisory provision. In the first place, perhaps to an exaggerated extent, the men of Vichy were held to be untrustworthy; for, in spite of promises to the contrary, they had handed over to the conquerors four hundred captured pilots, many of them shot down by the R.A.F., and this provided the Germans with an unexpected bonus in their preparation for the Battle of Britain. This was an act of Vichy malevolence which Churchill never forgot nor entirely forgave. More important still, the words of the Nazis had been proved over and over again to be utterly worthless. They would, forsooth, promise not to use the ships for their own purposes. 'What is the value of that?' said Churchill in the House of Commons, 'Ask half a dozen countries what is the value of such a solemn assurance.' It was a question to which all who had lived during the preceding seven years could give but one reply.

The War Cabinet reached the only possible conclusion. The ships at Plymouth, Portsmouth and Alexandria presented no insuperable difficulty, and if their crews chose to return to France no obstacle need be put in their way; but a wide range of options must be offered to Admiral Gensoul at Oran. The die was cast. By nightfall on 3rd July, when Gensoul had rejected all the options open to him and the reluctant Somerville had opened fire, a major part of the French Navy was disabled, sunk or in British hands. Churchill, deeply distressed by the decision he had asked his colleagues to take, said he did not see how Britain could avoid being at war with France on the morrow. Nor could he be quite sure how the House of Commons and the British public would receive the dire news.

He need not have worried. When on the following afternoon he gave his account to Parliament, he ended it with the words: 'I leave the judgment of our action, with confidence, to Parliament. I leave it to the nation, and I leave it to the United States. I leave it to the world and to history.'

History has a way of judging by the light, prejudices and knowledge of later days: Parliament and the nation judged by their own immediate sentiments. After hearing the speech in the House of Commons, I recorded in my diary: 'He told the whole story of Oran and the House listened enthralled and amazed. Gasps of surprise were audible but it was clear that the action taken was unanimously approved. When the speech was over all the members rose to their feet, waved their Order Papers and cheered loudly. Winston left the House visibly affected. I heard him say to Hore Belisha: "This is heartbreaking for me." '

The United States Administration now saw that the British were seriously determined to continue the struggle. One evening at Chequers, in the following January, Mr Harry Hopkins told me it was Oran which convinced President Roosevelt, in spite of opinions to the contrary sent by Ambassador Joseph P. Kennedy, that the British really would go on fighting, as Churchill had promised, if necessary for years, if necessary alone. Thenceforward it was the President's primary interest to see how, in spite of Congressional doubts, all assistance short of war could be made available to the United Kingdom. Throughout the entire world it became clear that the British had burned not merely the French boats but their own: the vision of a total and immediate victory for Nazi Germany, so vivid in June 1940, already began to seem a trifle blurred in July.

John Colville

Foreword

I have based this story on the personal experiences of survivors and on the Cabinet and Admiralty papers now in the Public Record Office. I have also had access to the French Commander-in-Chief's reports and depositions and other material from the French side.

The facts, therefore, in so far as I can ascertain them, are as reported in French and British official and semi-official documents. I should perhaps add that where dialogue occurs in this drama, it is not invented by me but is based on reports made at the time by the protagonists in which the actual conversations are recorded.

The Deadly Stroke

Chapter 1

On Sunday, 30th June 1940, a newly assembled British Fleet lay in the harbour of Gibraltar preparing for action. Across the bay the lights of neutral Spain twinkled as Force H replenished with oil, ammunition, food and stores. In the Fleet and in Gibraltar itself specialised activities were being pressed ahead with all despatch. Everyone, in the phrase of the day, was 'flat out'. But why? What was it all about?

That evening Vice-Admiral Sir James Somerville, Flag Officer Force H, called a meeting of his senior officers to brief them on the operation ahead. They met in the Admiral's day cabin of the battlecruiser HMS *Hood*. To begin with, since Force H had not so far come together as a fleet, and very few people knew what was expected of them, the temper of the meeting seemed brisk and full of expectation. This was a high-powered gathering of naval talent. Attendance comprised 'Nutty' Wells, the Vice-Admiral Commanding Aircraft Carriers (who privately considered he should have had command of Force H himself), Vice-Admiral Sir Dudley North, the Flag Officer at Gibraltar who had command of the North Atlantic and Western Mediterranean stations in both of which areas Force H was to become the striking force, and Captain Cedric – 'Hooky' – Holland, R.N., Captain of HMS *Ark Royal*, who was being seconded for the most difficult task he had been given in the whole of his naval career.

Also present were the Captains of the battleships *Resolution* and *Valiant*, the Captains of the cruisers *Arethusa* and *Enterprise*, the Captains (D) of the 8th and 13th Destroyer Flotillas and the various specialist staff officers, on whose preparatory work the success of the forthcoming operation would largely depend.

Somerville got down to essentials right away.

'The code name of this operation is "Catapult" and its object is to prevent the French warships at Oran, and possibly also at Algiers, from falling into the hands of the enemy,' he began, referring to the rough operation orders which had already been drafted. 'The main French Fleet is at present at Oran with cruisers at Algiers and Sfax and small units at Bizerta. Under the terms of the recent armistice we understand that ships are to be delivered to French metropolitan ports for demilitarising under enemy control. The French, however, appear to be hoping they will be allowed to retain and demilitarise their ships in French colonial ports. The main Italian fleet is believed to be in the Taranto area with light forces on the east coasts of Italy and Sicily. Submarines and aircraft are available to operate in the western basin of the Mediterranean, the nearest Italian aerodrome being about 300 miles from Oran.

'The Spanish attitude is uncertain and is liable to turn against us, in which case the use of Gibraltar as a base would probably be denied us. The Med. fleet working from Alexandria may synchronise operations in the Central Mediterranean with ours in the western basin. There are two Med. fleet submarines *Proteus* and *Pandora* patrolling off Oran and Algiers respectively and flying boats from Gibraltar will also be operating.'

By now initial anticipation had sobered down into uneasy silence. 'To carry out my intention,' the Admiral went on, 'persuasion and threat will be used as expedient. I am ordered to inform the French that they must either bring their ships to British harbours and fight with us, steam with reduced crews to a British or West Indian port from which their crews would be repatriated, demilitarise their ships immediately to our satisfaction or scuttle them.'

He paused as the effect of this sank in. No one moved.

'Should the French be unwilling to adopt any of the above measures, it will then be necessary to show that we are in earnest by offensive action without endangering French ships. If that doesn't work we must then destroy the French ships by our own action.'

The full horror of what they were about to do to their erstwhile comrades now gripped the assembled officers. No one coughed or moved and there was an attentive hush in the Admiral's cabin with its blue baize table cloth and its portraits of King George the Sixth and Queen Elizabeth looking down on them.

'My delegate, Captain Holland, will take passage in HMS *Foxhound* to Oran, arriving at about 0700 on Wednesday, the 3rd July. *Foxhound* will subsequently act under the orders of Captain Holland who will then carry out the special instructions issued to him which I will summarise as follows. The French *must* carry out one of the measures referred to. Scuttling may be undertaken either inside or outside the harbour. If such necessary action is not in progress by 1400, we will proceed to destroy their ships ourselves. If that occurs we cannot hold ourselves responsible for any loss of life in ships in the harbour or ashore in close proximity to the harbour.'

Everyone present visualised the execution of these orders and continued to listen in appalled silence.

'During these negotiations,' the Admiral went on, '*Foxhound* will endeavour to report progress and the French reaction. In the interests of her own security she may, however, withdraw, leaving the delegates behind if necessary.'

Instinctively all eyes turned on the gaunt features of Hooky Holland. He had the least enviable task of all, especially if he should be left behind when the action began.

'The remainder of Force H will arrive off Oran at about 0900, *Ark Royal* providing air reconnaissance of the harbours of Oran and Mers-el-Kebir. She will also provide reconnaissance to seaward, fighter patrols for her own protection and A/S patrols for herself and the battle squadron as arranged by Vice-Admiral Aircraft Carriers.'

Attention switched to Admiral Wells whose sharp tongue and aggressive personality carried their own guarantee of friction. Like Holland, he gave no indication of what was going through his mind.

'Should we learn that French surface units have left harbour during the night, aircraft from *Ark Royal* will locate and shadow them.'

The old 'string bags' of the Fleet Air Arm were going to be busy, but at that stage of the war, naval air power was still regarded as an adjunct rather than as a principal offensive weapon. It was the big guns which mattered, as they had done in the First World War.

'So much for the initial phase of the operation,' Somerville continued dryly. 'The second phase will be to show the French that we are in earnest. This will consist of firing a few rounds or the dropping of bombs close to, but not actually hitting French ships. *Hood* should be prepared to fire a few salvoes just clear of Mers-el-Kebir harbour and *Ark Royal* will carry out a bombing attack on the harbour itself, taking care to avoid hitting the ships.'

Normally at this point someone would have risked a *sotto voce* wisecrack aimed at the Gunnery Officers present. To avoid hitting a target should not be too difficult a feat. Today, though, every face was glum and no one spoke.

'The next and final stage is when and if it becomes necessary to destroy or sink the French ships. Priorities here are first the *Strasbourg* and *Dunkerque*, secondly the older battleships *Bretagne* and *Provence*, and then other fighting ships in order of size. Methods of destruction will largely depend on circumstances which cannot be foreseen such as weather, smoke, French reaction, etc. If the French offer organised and spirited resistance, we may need to develop a full offensive on French ships and shore batteries with all the means at our disposal. In this case the code word ANVIL will be signalled to all our forces. Senior Officers are then to take all necessary action to crush the resistance, ceasing fire as soon as it is apparent that the French are no longer resisting. Screening destroyers are not to leave the screen unless so directed.'

The lesson in annihilation continued, much as if a surgeon had been explaining to medical students how to excise a malignant tumour. Somerville's audience remained receptive and grim.

'If, on the other hand,' the firm voice went on, 'no organised French resistance is encountered, the destruction of French ships will be undertaken with more deliberation and greater economy of ammunition and torpedoes, available reserves of which are at present very limited. The procedure adopted will depend largely on conditions and each individual attack will be ordered by signal. In Mers-el-Kebir long range gunfire by main armament of capital ships, with aircraft spotting, will be ordered to destroy morale, damage anti-aircraft equipment and induce French crews to abandon their ships. Bombing by aircraft from *Ark Royal* will also be employed, followed by the sinking of those ships still afloat by special demolition parties from two destroyers of the 13th Destroyer Flotilla . . . and that's about all except, of course, that if we encounter the Italian Fleet we shall at once engage them, deferring operations on the French as necessary. Detailed orders will be in your hands tomorrow. Now let's deal with any questions you may want to ask.'

Long naval training ensured that none of them embarked on a criticism of the operation itself. 'Catapult' had been ordered and the task, however ghastly, would have to be carried out. Professional comment on different aspects of the operation, however, was both necessary and desirable.

'Torpedo attack by aircraft will be difficult and unproductive,' Vice-Admiral Wells remarked, 'unless anti-aircraft gunfire is first silenced.'

'And net defences in a restricted harbour rule out torpedo attack by destroyers,' one of the Captains (D) added.

Thus a general discussion began. It was finally decided that a round or two should be fired at Mers-el-Kebir – but not aimed to hit. This would demonstrate that the British were in earnest. If this failed to bring acceptance of the terms, a limited period of gunfire and/or bombing would be used to cause evacuation of the ships, final sinking being effected by either torpedo bomber or demolition according to circumstances.

Complete destruction by gunfire would require a great deal of ammunition and bring about a very serious loss of life. For the same reason, in the case of Oran itself as opposed to the more open harbour of Mers-el-Kebir, it was agreed that gunfire would cause very severe civilian casualties. It was hoped that the action taken at Mers-el-Kebir would induce the French in Oran to scuttle their ships.

'What are the chances of the French using force to resist our demands?' someone asked.

'I would say it's highly improbable,' Somerville answered, 'especially in their present state of morale. But perhaps you'd comment on that, Hooky, from your time as Naval Attaché in Paris and your more recent experience over there.'

Holland looked down at some notes he had made.

'The present complex attitude of the French Navy,' he said, 'makes it almost impossible to draw any firm conclusions. A week ago I was in Casablanca where I had interviews with three French Admirals and various officers on their staffs. Both Admirals Ollive and de Laborde said they thought not only could the British never win the war but also that the only thing left for us to do was make the best peace terms we could as soon as possible. De Laborde said blockade was our only effective weapon but in his opinion it would never achieve its aim. When I said the Empire would fight to the last man and that we were not only determined to win the war but convinced we could do so, they merely shrugged their shoulders, expressed a dubious hope that we might be right but were evidently quite unimpressed by what I said.'

He paused for a moment, recalling the French officers he was talking about.

'With Admiral Ollive this attitude is understandable. He is old, weak and in no sense a leader. With de Laborde the case is different. He is a strong man, very reserved, has never meddled with politics, a Royalist but a patriotic one in that he works for the country's good. He is also intensely loyal to Darlan, who went over his head to become Chief of the Naval Staff, and thus de Laborde makes it a point of honour to show his loyalty by every possible means.'

'Who is the French Admiral at Oran?' somebody asked.

'Gensoul – and I'll come to him in a minute. To finish off my

Casablanca visit, I had a meeting with Admiral Moreau on very different lines. He is an old friend of mine and more open and broad-minded than so many Frenchmen. If he had been in a more senior position, I think he would have gone on fighting. The point of view he gave me as being the most general French one was that France had signed an armistice and had not made peace. When they had pulled themselves together and the right moment had come, we would again find them fighting by our side. He said he was certain we should find many officers trying to get away to fight with us. He was convinced there was a strong party working in France to loosen the German stranglehold on the country, to start sabotage and to pull the country together.'

Again he paused momentarily to consider these implications.

'Thus I got mixed answers from three different senior officers when I asked if the French Navy would not join up and continue to fight with us. I'm sure many of the more junior officers were ready to fight on.'

'What are the main factors affecting them at the moment?' another questioner asked.

'Briefly, I'd say, in descending order of importance – uncertainty as to what brutal action the Germans would take against the wives and families of those who fought on. That's the prime factor. Then there's the mental paralysis of many of the older officers brought on by the collapse of the army and the invasion of France.'

'What about their feelings towards us?'

'I think there's a certain resentment and antagonism on account of having failed us. The French are touchy, a psychological fact we frequently overlook, and this helps to inflame a deep-seated feeling of inferiority. The French Navy has been through many lean years. Most French naval officers are well read. They feel keenly their Navy's fall from the first rank. It was not until about 1935 that a move was made to rebuild the French Navy and to impress on France that this was necessary if the Empire was to be held. During the years 1937, 1938 and 1939 it was possible to see the growing importance that the

Navy held in the eyes of the public. This has become more and more the case during the war and the Navy has risen in its own estimation. The Navy hasn't been contaminated by the panic and flight in France. It fought well at Dunkirk and Calais.'

'Why hasn't Darlan come away and taken the Navy with him?'

'I have no answer to that and I know Darlan reasonably well. He's ambitious. He could certainly do it. If he did, I've no doubt he would spring into the limelight of history as a great leader. He hates the Germans personally. He's very proud of his unique position as Admiral of the Fleet. The centralisation of command of all sea forces in the person of the Chief of the Naval Staff has always been very marked, although Darlan has often been at pains to assure me otherwise. I imagine, therefore, that all senior officers are awaiting orders from their Chief.'

'And Gensoul?'

Holland paused for a moment and frowned.

'In my opinion he's correct – completely service. He'll never step out of line. He's also, perhaps, somewhat pigheaded.' He paused, weighing his words, and then went on, slightly hesitantly, 'I don't know him well. He was described to me as a little overfull of his own importance – something of a small man in a big position.' He shrugged his shoulders. 'Well, we shall see. My own experience in dealing with the French is that intellectual persuasion, not force, is the best method of gaining one's end.'

At this there was a spontaneous murmur of approval and the meeting concluded. Later Somerville was to write in his report, 'Admiral North, Vice-Admiral Wells and Captain Holland all expressed themselves as strongly opposed to the use of force. They considered that there was little fear of the French allowing their ships to fall into German hands.'

How did it all come about? How was it that for the first time in a hundred and twenty-five years, the Royal Navy fired upon the French, their comrades of a few days before? By what bizarre chain of events did the tragedy of Mers-el-Kebir take place in that scorching July of 1940?

In writing, thirty years later, about that summer of 1940, the big words – the superlatives – seem to have lost their meaning, mainly through over-use. Perhaps understatement is now a better way in which to make that violent time intelligible. But how do you understate a cataclysm, the dictionary definition of which is a 'deluge . . . political or social upheaval'? Because the German deluge which began to pour over Europe on 10th May 1940 and which culminated in the fall of France was certainly cataclysmic in its effect and both the political and social upheavals were so great that nothing could ever be quite as it had been before.

No scale of measurement, no values remained unaltered. The war which Hitler had initiated on 1st September 1939 and which had then seemed to peter away, suddenly flared up, like a sheet of petrol ignited on the top of the sea, and after burning with a ferocity rarely if ever seen before in the history of the world, achieved its purpose – or the greater part of its purpose – in six to seven weeks.

As recently as May 1940 nothing very startling had happened to England or France. Eight months of the 'phoney war', even allowing for the invasion of Poland, Denmark and Norway, had lulled people into believing the propaganda they had ingested. Hitler really was bluffing and had been all along. Were not the Germans desperately short of rubber, oil and other essentials? They would eventually be starved into submission. We were bound to win.

The Royal Navy had control of the seas. The Maginot line was impregnable. Economically no shoddy German dictator could seriously pit himself against the might and resources of the French and British Empires, let alone the United States of America, and hope to come out on top. It was only a question of time.

It was indeed. Before Hitler opened his blitzkrieg on Holland, Belgium and France, Neville Chamberlain, still unable to believe that he had been one hundred per cent wrong in his assessment of the German leader and his policy of appeasement, had been conducting the British war effort with all the detachment and inspiration of a Borough Treasurer.

Across the Channel, General Weygand and Marshal Pétain were neither of them in the French Government nor even themselves in metropolitan France. Weygand was Commander-in-Chief, Near East at Beirut. Pétain pottered about as the French Ambassador to Franco's Spain.

Ordinary people were discontented and uneasy but by and large the life we had all known for the last twenty years – since, in fact, the world had settled down after the holocaust of the 'Great' War – continued much as before. Then suddenly everything, as in a volcanic eruption, seemed to happen at once.

The changes began on 9th May. Chamberlain, already dying of cancer, was dismissed by the British Parliament in the terrible words of Cromwell . . . 'You have sat here too long for any good you have been doing. Depart, I say, let us have done with you. In the name of God – go!' Churchill moved from the Admiralty to Downing Street and a new era began. At last a world leader had emerged. The moment had indeed engendered the man.

That same night Hitler left in his special train for the front, having despatched a brief telegram to the Dutch Government informing them that the Wehrmacht would be with them in a matter of hours. The blitzkrieg had started but the huge guns of the Maginot fortifications remained silent since the German Army simply went round them. No one in England sang, 'We're going to hang up the washing on the Siegfried Line,' any more.

As far back as January 1940, Churchill, then First Lord of the Admiralty, had said to Admiral Sir Dudley Pound, the First Sea Lord, in a moment of exasperation: 'Our army is puny as far as the fighting front is concerned: our Air Force is hopelessly inferior to the Germans' . . . we maintain an attitude of complete passivity, dispersing our forces ever more widely . . . do you realise that perhaps we are headed for *defeat*?'

It was ominously true. But no one paid much attention to Churchill in those wilderness days. The downhill course of indecision and apathy continued until he became Prime Minister and then, in the opinion of the world, it was already too late.

Meanwhile, if England stagnated under Chamberlain, things were considerably worse in France. Uncertainty, complacency and treason coloured the political life of the great nation on whom the land defence of the West depended and poisoned France's relationship with the outside world.

On 21st March Daladier and his government resigned, to be replaced two days later by Paul Reynaud, at that time the nearest equivalent to Churchill in France. Reynaud was greeted, when he presented his Cabinet to the French Chamber, 'without warmth, if not with hostility, by elements of right, left and centre'.

In his policy statement which preceded the vote of confidence and on which he was to rely, Reynaud said: 'Everything is at stake in this total war. Winning means saving everything: succumbing means losing everything . . . Parliament, expressing the feelings of the whole country, has fully taken stock of these dreadful facts. So the Government that sits before you has no other purpose, and desires no other purpose, than that of rousing, uniting and directing the nation's energies so as to fight and win, and of stamping out treason from whatever source. Thanks to your confidence and with your support, we shall accomplish this task.'

The French Chamber at that time numbered 535 Deputies. When the vote was taken, Reynaud came out of it with a majority of one. One hundred and eleven Deputies abstained. It was not a good augury for what was to follow, and what was to follow had already cast its shadow in advance.

On 10th January 1940 a German Staff plane had strayed into a snowstorm and made a forced landing in Belgium. The pilot tried to burn his papers but the Belgian police had seized a briefcase containing full details of the German line-up and its invasion plans. Belgian Intelligence at once passed these on to the Allies. Gamelin, the French Supreme Commander, brushed this off as a German trap. Churchill saw it, correctly, as a genuine accident. But Churchill was still only First Lord of the

Admiralty with but a lateral say in the running of the war. No changes were made in the French line of defence, and Belgium continued to refuse permission for French troops to man a forward line on its soil, which would at least have acted as an early-warning system.

On paper the Allies were undoubtedly stronger. But at day-break on 10th May, when every available German aircraft took to the air, the German answer to such a paper assessment comprised a column of tanks relentlessly pressing forward through the Ardennes forest and stretching back over a hundred miles. Then, when the French army advanced to what they imagined to be fortified Belgian territory, they found no trenches, no defence structures, no fixed auxiliary weapons, no anti-tank preparations, no earthworks – only 'Cointet' obstructions comprising trestles connected by coils of barbed wire set behind small anti-tank minefields. The surprise was complete and the subsequent rout inevitable.

France faced a new form of war and General Gamelin, who nine days later was to be relieved of his command, came rue-fully near the mark when he observed: 'There is no denying that we were in a strange pickle for a nation about to go into battle.'

A mere six days after the blitzkrieg began, the way to Paris lay wide open to the German army. The French Government decided to remove itself to Tours, the Quai d'Orsay was burning its most secret papers and President Roosevelt was offering the Royal Navy the shelter of American ports.

This offer, which surprised and 'took aback' the British Ambassador, nevertheless proved to be a sober reminder of the realities of the situation. In essence it was going to be sea-power – as it had been in the First World War – which would turn the balance at long last in favour of the Allies. Of this Churchill was fully aware.

The pace now accelerated into total disaster. Back in March the French Government at their own suggestion had solemnly bound themselves in consort with the British not to make a separate peace. Opponents of this were quick to point out that such an undertaking was incompatible with equity and 'could only be arrived at after a complete agreement as to the terms and conditions for peace and the sacrifices each country would accept in order to win the war'.

But Reynaud was not then dealing with Churchill, whose fighting determination had never been in doubt, but with Chamberlain, who was synonymous in the French view with 'Munich' and 'appeasement'. So the fact that the French entered the war with over one hundred divisions whereas the British Expeditionary Force contributed a mere five to the common cause was not brought into the negotiations until that common cause was on the point of collapse. By then it was too late.

From Tours the French Government moved to Bordeaux on the very day that the Germans entered Paris. By now Pétain had been recalled from Madrid and General Weygand had taken over the supreme direction of the war on land. Churchill flew back and forth from France making continuous endeavours to keep some sort of fighting spirit alive in the French Government and High Command. He was not to succeed.

By this time Dunkirk had come and gone and a certain faction in the French Government wished to solicit an armistice. Inevitably the problem of the French Fleet and its disposal began nudging its way to the top of any proposed armistice agenda. Moreover, the French Fleet, and François Darlan, its dynamic Admiral of the Fleet, whose hatred of the Germans only just exceeded his distaste for the British, was brought up with increasing frequency in the British, French, German and Italian councils of war. It was also present in American thinking.

As early as 26th May, before the evacuation of Dunkirk, the President of the United States had cabled his Ambassador in Paris to say that: 'while we still hope the invasion will be checked; if the worst comes to the worst, we regard the retention of the French Fleet as a force in being as vital to the reconstitution of France and of the French colonies and to the ultimate control of the Atlantic and other oceans and as a vital influence towards getting less harsh terms of peace. This means that the French Fleet must not get caught bottled up in the

Mediterranean. . . . Finally, if the Germans hold out alluring offers to France based on the surrender of the French Fleet, it should be remembered that these offers are of no ultimate value and that the condition of France could be no worse but in fact could be far stronger if the Fleet were removed as a whole to safe places.'

To this Ambassador Bullitt replied: 'I believe as strongly as I have ever believed anything that you will be unable to protect the United States from German attack unless you have the co-operation of the French and British fleets. I believe that one of the surest ways to obtain such co-operation would be by sending our Atlantic Fleet to the Mediterranean.'

Three days later, on 29th May, he cabled in even stronger terms: 'It is now or never for the United States. If you can send your Atlantic Fleet to Tangier and inform Mussolini that you are doing so after the Fleet has sailed, he will not dare to strike. Otherwise he will strike, and in a very few months you will face a joint attack by Germany, Italy and Japan alone.' The American Fleet was not sent to Tangier.

A similar assessment was arrived at by Darlan, who wrote a confidential memorandum in his own hand to Admiral Le Luc, his Chief of Staff, saying that . . . 'should military events lead to an armistice with conditions imposed by the Germans and should these conditions include the surrender of the Fleet, I do not intend to carry out this order.'

Such a valuable document was not of course available to Churchill but a fortnight later, on 12th June, he was given a verbal promise by the French Admiral of the Fleet. On one of his visits to the French Government at Tours, he drew Darlan to one side and said: 'I hope you will never surrender the Fleet.'

'There is no question of doing so,' Darlan answered. 'It would be contrary to our naval traditions and honour. We shall never hand over to Germany or Italy. Orders to scuttle will be given in the event of danger.'

Strangely enough this accorded with the Führer's thinking. In June 1940, surprising as it may seem, Hitler wanted peace. He had no wish to destroy the British Empire but intended it to remain in being under German control since, like the Roman Catholic church, he regarded it as an essential stabilising factor in world affairs. On 18th June, when he and Ribbentrop met Mussolini at Munich, he not only made this clear but insisted that the French be offered moderate armistice terms so that the French Fleet would not join the British. The best thing, he added, would be for France to scuttle it.

But this was not to be known until after the war. Five days before this meeting, on 13th June and the day before the Germans entered Paris, General Weygand was urging on the French Cabinet the immediate cessation of hostilities. To this a tired and exasperated Reynaud replied that they must await an answer to the latest proposals made to the President of the United States. Weygand then said: 'Let us at least make use of the interval to safeguard the French Fleet by sending it to North African ports. In my view all such measures should be taken before embarking on armistice negotiations with the enemy.'

It was perhaps at this point that Darlan's attitude hardened and a train of events began which came to a climax at Mers-el-Kebir. A Corsican named Campinchi was then the Minister of Marine. He was in political control of the French Navy over Darlan in the same way as in England the First Lord of the Admiralty, who was a politician, was in control of the First Sea Lord who was an Admiral on the Active List.

'What is the point of seeking an armistice,' Campinchi said to the French Cabinet, 'if the Government is determined not to hand over the Fleet? That is a condition the Germans are bound to impose.'

This statement was backed up by two other Ministers, Messrs Monnet and Rio, who observed that negotiating an armistice would inevitably lead to placing the Fleet at Germany's disposal and that 'that would mean forfeiting our honour'.

At this Weygand burst into a rage and said: 'There is no question of that. There can never be any question of handing over any part of our Fleet. I should be the first to reject the armistice if that condition were imposed by Germany.'

35

To this Darlan coldly retorted: 'The matter is my responsibility and I have already given formal undertakings on the subject.'

It was not Darlan's responsibility – or at least only partially so at that time – but he was soon to have it his way and such was the personality of the little Gascon who, almost single-handed, had built up the French Navy into the force it was, that in a few short days Campinchi was to disappear from the scene and Darlan to combine the office of Admiral of the Fleet with that of Minister of Marine. He thus took the supreme naval power of France into his hands. But by then the armistice had been signed and the die was cast.

London and Washington were not dealing with Paris but with a French Government on the run and in the last stages of collapse. Communications went astray. Panic reigned. Misunderstandings – some of them hinging on the exact meaning of French and English words – and misjudgments resulted. In such a climate of disaster, it is remarkable not that mistakes were made but that so few of them had any real effect on the course of events. One of these misjudgments, however, was to be significant and it was this which contributed to the débâcle of Mers-el-Kebir.

The 16th of June 1940 was certainly an extraordinary day in both London and Bordeaux. The previous evening, after a stormy meeting in which both Reynaud and the President of the Republic, Monsieur Lebrun, had threatened to resign, the 'defeatist faction' (in Churchill's phrase) of Weygand and Pétain won the day. They wanted an end to the fighting and a message was despatched to the British Government asking their consent to the French enquiring of the Germans as to the terms of an armistice.

The British answer was phoned through to its Ambassador in Bordeaux the next morning and immediately passed to the French premier. It was that the British would accept the French request, 'on condition that the French Fleet was placed beyond German power – in fact that it should be directed to British ports'.

Concurrently with this, however, a revolutionary proposal was being drafted that morning in London which, at any rate in the British view, was to dwarf all other business in importance. This was an offer of 'an indissoluble union' between France and Great Britain. A final decision to offer this union, however, was not taken by the British War Cabinet until the afternoon of the 16th.

At eleven o'clock in the morning at Bordeaux 'the distracted Council of Ministers met again, [in Churchill's account] President Lebrun being present. The President of the Senate, M. Jeanneney, was brought in to endorse, both on his own behalf and on that of his colleague, the President of the Chamber, M. Herriot, the proposal of the Premier to transfer the Government to North Africa. Up rose Marshal Pétain and read a letter, which it is believed had been written for him by another hand, resigning from the Cabinet. Having finished his speech, he prepared to leave the room.

He was persuaded by the President of the Republic to remain on condition that an answer would be given him during the day. The Marshal had also complained of the delay in asking for an armistice. Reynaud replied that if one asked an ally to free one from an obligation it was customary to await an answer. The session then closed. After luncheon the Ambassador brought to Reynaud the textual answer of the British Government of which he had already given the telephoned purport in his conversation of the morning.

This text was as follows:

Foreign Office to Sir R. Campbell. Please give M. Reynaud the following message, which has been approved by the Cabinet. Mr Churchill to M. Reynaud 16 June 1940. 12.35 p.m.:

'Our agreement forbidding separate negotiations, whether for armistice or peace, was made with the French Republic, and not with any particular French Administration or statesman. It therefore involves the honour of France. Nevertheless, provided but only provided that the French Fleet is sailed forthwith for British harbours pending negotiations, His Majesty's Government give their full consent to an enquiry by the French Government to ascertain the terms of an armistice for France. His Majesty's Government, being resolved to continue the war, wholly exclude themselves from all part in the above-mentioned enquiry concerning an armistice.'

Later that afternoon, at 3.10 p.m., whilst the British War Cabinet was again in session and deeply engaged in drafting the terms of the proposed Franco-British union, the Foreign Office despatched a further message to the British Ambassador at Bordeaux which expanded the previous decision.

You should inform M. Reynaud as follows, [the Foreign Office said]: We expect to be consulted as soon as any armistice terms are received. This is necessary not merely in virtue of treaty forbidding separate peace or armistice, but also in view of vital consequences of any armistice to ourselves, having regard especially to the fact that British troops are fighting with French Army. You should impress on French Government that in stipulating for removal of French Fleet to British ports we have in mind French interests as well as our own, and are convinced that it will strengthen the hands of the French Government in any armistice discussions if they can show that the French Navy is out of reach of the German forces. . . .

I have gone into these preliminaries at length since they set the scene for what was to follow. With due allowance for hindsight and a certain amount of wordiness, nothing perhaps shows more clearly than this message the basic divergence in thinking between the two governments at that time. Moreover timing and difficulties in communication, which sound an undertone throughout this story, now became of growing importance.

In view of the extraordinary and dramatic offer of union about to be made to the French, and uncertainties as to how it would be received, the British War Cabinet thought it politic to suspend action on British agreement to the French demand for an armistice. Whether these tactics were sound or not is a matter of opinion. The hope was that such a demand would not then be made.

A telegram was therefore sent to the British Ambassador asking him to delay presentation of the two previous messages. This was an unfair, and in the event an impossible responsibility to put on the man on the spot. The import of the messages had already been conveyed verbally and, indeed, by the time this telegram arrived the messages themselves had been given to the French premier. Reynaud had not taken them well and had gone off in a dejected mood.

A messenger was therefore sent after him to say that the two earlier messages should be considered 'cancelled'. As Churchill observes, 'suspended' would have been a better word. But on 16th June 1940 there was little time for semantics. For all practical purposes, the French took the messages as cancelled and this action, overlooked in what followed, was later to be used by the French to substantiate their claim that the sailing of the French Fleet to British ports was no longer an integral part of British agreement to the seeking of an armistice.

As shown later in this story the proposed declaration of unity was curtly rejected by the Bordeaux government. Crisis built upon crisis and a few days later both the British Ambassador and General de Gaulle left France, not to return for another four years. The negotiation of an armistice, the resignation of both Reynaud and President Lebrun, and the assumption of power by Marshal Pétain and those of his persuasion, took up the following chaotic week. France was lost. Subsequent international opinion considered that it would be only a matter of time before Great Britain followed.

This, of course, was never Churchill's idea and the continuing and mounting British resistance was a sad disappointment to Hitler. Whilst both sides now faced an urgent rethinking of their respective strategies, the question of the French Fleet went into a sort of limbo. This might be all right so far as Hitler and Mussolini were concerned: for England – and at one remove America – it was clear that other arrangements must at once be made. What resulted is the subject-matter of this book.

Chapter 2

It all began in London in a terrible rush. Less than a week before the Day, no such thing as Force H existed. In the afternoon of Thursday, 27th June, Commander Anthony Buzzard, R.N., a tall slim sandy-haired Navy tennis champion, had been sitting in the office of the Director of Plans at the Admiralty wondering if he would be able to get down to his home at Godalming for a few hours that coming weekend.

A couple of months before, he had had HMS *Ghurka*, a destroyer and his first seagoing command, sunk beneath him in a Norwegian fiord. A D.S.O. and a few days later, he had been brought back into the Plans Division of the Admiralty, the real brainbox of British sea-power, in which he had served from 1938 till the beginning of 1940.

Late that afternoon an incident occurred which he was to remember vividly the rest of his life. The door of the office, next to that of the First Sea Lord, opened abruptly and James Somerville put his head inside.

'Tony,' he said, 'you're sailing for the Med. tomorrow. We're taking passage to Gib. in *Arethusa*. Go home and get your whites. You're going to be my Staff Officer (Plans).'

So without further ado Buzzard turned over his papers to his assistant and then he and his wife spent the evening routing out from his Gieves tin trunks the white uniform he would need for the Mediterranean summer. The next day he had caught the 11 o'clock train from Waterloo still much in the dark as to what it was all about. As the train began to move, Buzzard looked out of the window and saw a stubby Paymaster Lieutenant Commander running along the platform, suitcase in hand and revolver and gas-mask banging at his side. A carriage door at the rear of the train was flung open and Bill Farrell, the Admiral's Secretary, scrambled aboard. Thus did these essential elements of the Force H staff leave for their new appointments.

Also in that train which reached Portsmouth an hour and a half later was Captain E. G. Jeffery, R.N., late of the Imperial Defence College and now to be Chief of Staff to the Flag Officer, Force H, together with his new secretary, Paymaster Lieutenant John Rennie, R.N., who, like Buzzard and the rest of them, had been co-opted the previous day.

Admiral Somerville had proceeded independently to Portsmouth as had his Flag Lieutenant and Signal Officer, Commander Keith Walter, R.N., but both were now there on the platform of Portsmouth Harbour Station. It was a fine sunny day and there was no air-raid alert, the silver barrage balloons floating serenely over the Royal Navy's principal dockyard. A few minutes later they were embarking on board the 5,000 ton cruiser detailed to take them to Gibraltar and at 1430 HMS *Arethusa* sailed, turning west in the Channel at 28 knots.

That same day de Gaulle, still a virtually unknown Tank officer, was recognised by the British Government as leader of the Free French. However, he was denied Churchill's confidence as to what was going to happen in five days' time. The previous afternoon in Washington, Mr Cordell Hull, the American Secretary of State, had told Lord Lothian, the British Ambassador, that it was the considered opinion of the United States Government that the British Fleet should be put in the shelter of American ports. In other words the British Isles were now being looked on as a strategic write-off.

This only increased Churchill's certainty that an arresting political gesture was immediately required. This gesture must demonstrate to the world that the British Prime Minister meant what he said after Dunkirk in what was, perhaps, the most dramatic and magnificently worded speech of his life . . . 'even though large tracts of Europe and many old and famous states have fallen or may fall into the grip of the Gestapo [which he pronounced Jest a Poe] and all the odious apparatus of

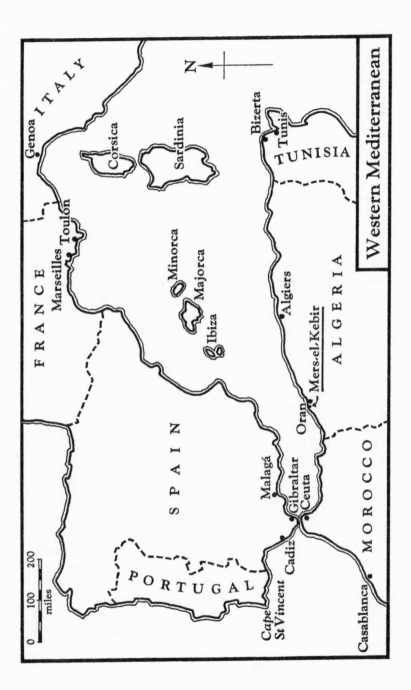

Western Mediterranean

N

FRANCE

Genoa

ITALY

Corsica

Sardinia

Marseilles Toulon

Minorca

Majorca

Ibiza

SPAIN

Bizerta

Tunis

TUNISIA

Algiers

Mers-el-Kebir

Oran

ALGERIA

Malagá

Gibraltar

Ceuta

Cadiz

Cape St Vincent

PORTUGAL

MOROCCO

Casablanca

0   100   200
miles

Nazi rule, we shall not flag nor fail. We shall go on to the end.'

This defiant heroism continued in phrases which were to light the spirit for the rest of the war.

'We shall fight in France, we shall fight on the seas and oceans, we shall fight with growing confidence and growing strength in the air: we shall defend our Island whatever the cost may be. We shall fight on the beaches, we shall fight on the landing grounds, we shall fight in the fields and in the streets, we shall fight in the hills: we shall never surrender and even if, which I do not for a moment believe, this Island or a large part of it were subjugated and starving, then our Empire beyond the seas, armed and guarded by the British Fleet, would carry on the struggle, until in God's good time, the New World with all its power and might, steps forth to the rescue and the liberation of the old.'

It was this fighting spirit which now, three weeks after that speech, appeared to be totally lacking in the French. Or was it? The realities were difficult to assess. There was de Gaulle. There was General Mittelhauser, the French Commander-in-Chief of the Middle Eastern theatre of war, who on 24th June, the day the armistice was signed, had publicly advocated continuing the fight. There was Georges Mandel, who with some twenty other Deputies had left for Casablanca in the cruiser *Massiglia* to set up an alternative Government – only to find himself arrested and held *incommunicado*.

There was Paul Reynaud, the tough French Premier, who had to the very last moment brought all the pressure he could to bear on his colleagues to fight on, but who was now no longer Prime Minister of France and who that very night was to be involved in a near fatal car crash.

Above all there was Admiral of the Fleet François Darlan, Commander-in-Chief of the French Navy, who in a single signal of a few short words could rally the world's fourth largest fleet to the allied cause and thus alter the whole course of the war. But what was to happen if such a signal was not forthcoming? That was the nub. It was with this situation that the small staff of officers and men, with their highly specialised skills, was now en route to Gibraltar to deal.

Behind the scenes a number of other things had been happening during the week before Force H was brought into being; all of them having a direct or indirect effect on the French Navy. The armistice terms which General Keitel handed to the French in the railway carriage at Compiègne on that grim hot day of 21st June stated in Article 8 that:

'The French war fleet, with the exception of that portion which is left at the disposal of the French Government to safe-guard its interests in its colonial empire, will be assembled in harbours to be determined, and demobilised and disarmed under the control of Germany and Italy respectively. The selection of these harbours will be based on the ships' home ports in peacetime.'

The directive thus set out was explicit and its object plain. However, the Teutonic mind which drafted the armistice terms must have been consciously or unconsciously aware that such a bald demand might be too much for even the shocked and stricken French leaders to accept and the pill was then sugared in the manner which Hitler had so successfully employed up to the outbreak of war.

'The German Government solemnly declares,' the terms went on, 'that during the war it does not intend to use for its own purposes the French War Fleet stationed in ports under Ger-man control, apart from units needed for coast-guarding and minesweeping. It further declares, solemnly and categorically, that it does not intend to stake any claims to the French Fleet on concluding the peace. Apart from that portion of the French War Fleet to be determined, which will be assigned to the task of protecting French interests in the colonial empire, all ships outside French territorial waters are to be recalled to France.'

It all depended on whether you believed Hitler's word of honour or not. That evening when General Huntziger, the chief French delegate, had telephoned General Weygand, the Supreme Commander-in-Chief, in Bordeaux, Weygand had asked, 'What about the Fleet?' General Huntziger had felt able to say, 'The Germans do not require it to be surrendered to them'; a statement which, with hindsight, is a little surprising – or perhaps naïve. It did not satisfy Darlan. In a signal that night to the Fleet he said, 'I hereby stipulate that, since nothing has yet been settled, hostilities are to continue.'

The next day the French High Command asked the German Armistice Commission to agree that French ships should be disarmed in North and West African ports and not in their pre-war home ports since a large proportion of the Fleet had been based on Cherbourg, Brest or l'Orient which would lie in the Occupied Zone.

The official German reply to this was devious. There was no need to insert the suggested amendment in the actual agreement, they said. The Germans did not refuse to accept the proposal but they considered it 'a practical measure' to be submitted to the Armistice Commission. This was later interpreted by a distinguished French Admiral to mean that: '. . . for reasons of prestige and *amour propre* that are readily understood, as victors they were unwilling to alter the original wording of their *Diktat* but fundamentally they were acceding to the request of the French Admiralty'.

The British saw it very differently. They were far more suspicious. Discussing it with Churchill, General Spears, who had lately been the British Prime Minister's special liaison officer with the French Government, said bluntly, 'If the Germans decide later on that they need the French Fleet, they will take it by the simple expedient of saying to the French: "Unless you hand over your ships intact, we will fire Marseilles. If that doesn't persuade you, we will set alight to Lyons and, if you still refuse, we will destroy Paris."' In view of Hitler's order four years later to burn Paris before the Allies could take back the city – an order so very nearly effected – there was a certain validity in this thinking, though this again could only be proved at a later date. At the time all those competent to judge and to make decisions were groping in the dark.

The next day, before the armistice had been accepted, the British Consuls in Tunis, Algiers and Rabat called upon the French Governors and the Resident-General, as they had done three days before, to urge them to break away from metropolitan France and to continue the fight. This time full naval, military and financial assistance was promised. The answer was a curt refusal and the consuls were again sent packing.

On Sunday, 23rd June, whilst the armistice terms were awaiting the formality of Italian agreement, it became known to Admiral Odend'hal, who was Head of the French Naval Mission in London, that the seizing of French merchant ships and the blockading of the French coastline was under active consideration by the British Admiralty. He signalled to Admiral Darlan in Bordeaux: 'British Government still unfamiliar with wording of naval clauses signed. Fully familiar only with original German wording communicated by its Ambassador. Is afraid of seeing our Fleet, once disarmed, fall into enemy hands and used against us. Can you instruct me?'

To this Darlan replied: 'All provisions accepted are conditioned by the fact that the French Fleet will definitely remain French, under the French flag, in French ports with French skeleton crews. These conditions do not endanger British interests. On the other hand the attitude of the British authorities that you report can only be viewed as unfriendly. Insist that measures contemplated are hastily called off.'

The rift was widening. There was now no British Ambassador in France (he had left the night before) and the B.B.C. had broadcast: 'the British Government find that the terms of the armistice just signed, in contravention of agreements solemnly made between the Allied Governments, reduce the Bordeaux Government to a state of complete subjection to the enemy and deprive it of all liberty and of all right to represent free French citizens. H.M. Government now declare that they can no longer regard the Bordeaux Government as the government of an independent country.'

The same day King George the Sixth cabled to President Lebrun: 'I learn with deep anxiety and dismay that your

Government under the cruel pressure of these tragic days contemplate sending the French Fleet to North African ports where it would be in evident danger of falling into hostile hands. I need not remind you, *Monsieur le Président*, should this occur how great would be the danger involved to our common cause and I rely on the solemn and explicit assurances already given to my Government that in no circumstances would your Government assent to any conditions that involved this consequence.'

In the meantime Monsieur Corbin, the French Ambassador in London, had resigned, the British Consuls in Tunis, Algiers and Rabat had been abruptly asked to leave and de Gaulle, in a speech at the French Lycée in London had set up the Free French National Committee. The British Government announced they would recognise this Committee 'so long as it continued to represent all French elements resolved to fight the common enemy'.

On Monday, 24th June, President Lebrun replied to King George: 'In the midst of the cruel events that my country is experiencing, after exhausting the final possibilities of military resistance to the invasion of which it has borne the brunt almost entirely with its own forces, I can only remind Your Majesty of the repeated assurances given by my Government to the British Government that the French War Fleet will not be able to be used against Great Britain. I like to hope that these assurances are likely to keep Your Majesty's Government to the path of friendship along which my country wishes to be able to persevere.'

There was little comfort to the British in the 'repeated assurances' referred to since what bankers call collateral support was ominously missing. In any case Monsieur Lebrun would soon no longer be the President of France.

A more cogent and moving message was sent to Churchill by Reynaud, the French Prime Minister. 'I appeal to your friendship and to the trust that you have always shown in me. Nothing would delight Hitler more than a permanent political quarrel between our two countries. Your speech yesterday so affected me that I have discussed it with Marshal Pétain . . .

the stipulations of the armistice agreement on the subject of the Fleet are admittedly liable to cause you concern. But I have just questioned Admiral Darlan on the subject in the presence of Marshal Pétain. Darlan states that when the terms relating to this measure are discussed before the armistice commission, steps will be taken to ensure that the enemy will in no circumstances be able to use our Fleet against Britain . . . this should reassure you in the matter. . . .'

It was possibly Commander Buzzard's calculations in the Plans Division of the Admiralty which brought matters to a head and it was ironic that Buzzard should now be 'on the business end' of the decisions inevitably reached. From the end of 1937 until the beginning of 1940, Buzzard was the 'Shipbuilder and Planner' to the Director of Plans. The Director of Plans in the Admiralty is the key man in naval preparations for war. Tom Phillips, his boss, may not have been very popular, particularly with the seagoing Admirals who had to execute Board of Admiralty decisions, but he was very competent indeed. He was virtually the brains of the Admiralty.

Buzzard was the Commander in the Plans Division responsible for each year's shipbuilding programme. In other words it was on his basic calculations that the Board of Admiralty decided what type and quantities of ships the Royal Navy would require in order to do its job. They tried to work to what was known as the 'two power standard' (thus bringing them into inevitable and continuous conflict with the Treasury, of course).

The two power standard meant that the Royal Navy must be able to take on and defeat the combined fleets of any two potential enemies at one and the same time. Buzzard had continuously to balance the power of every foreign battle fleet so that the various dispositions of the Royal Navy could always contain its enemies if war broke out.

Naval power in 1940 was based on capital ships. Battleships and their gun power were what mattered. So far as the Italian Fleet was concerned, the British reckoned it to be balanced by the French in the Mediterranean and this left Britain to settle Germany and if need be, Japan herself.

But what was to happen now that the French were disappearing off the map? The balance of power, in the phrase of the day, had gone for a Burton. This was why at the end of June 1940 the naval hierarchy, which consisted of the Director of Plans, the Vice Chief of the Naval Staff, the Naval Assistant to the First Sea Lord and finally the First Sea Lord himself found itself in a turmoil. With the French Fleet at risk all their calculations had gone wrong and they found themselves with nothing at the western end of the Mediterranean.

As things were they simply could not contain the Italian Fleet and since all the other myriad operations the Royal Navy undertook were under the umbrella of battleships, they had got to set up a battle fleet and base it on Gibraltar right away. And that was how Force H came about. The 'H' had no meaning, it was simply to throw enemy Intelligence off the scent.

During the passage to Gibraltar, Buzzard, Jeffery, the Chief of Staff, a highly-strung introspective officer who was later to hang himself in HMS *Renown*, the rest of the key staff and Admiral Somerville himself got out a rough and ready organisation to bring into being and administer their new fleet. It was not until the day after they had left the United Kingdom and were speeding south at nearly 30 knots that the War Cabinet finally made the harsh decision to put 'Operation Catapult' into execution.

On Saturday, 29th June 1940, the day before Somerville and his staff arrived at Gibraltar, the French Government left Bordeaux. Exhausted and deeply confused they set off piecemeal for the area of Clermont-Ferrand and Vichy in the centre of France.

During the cease-fire negotiations the Germans had agreed to Bordeaux being regarded as an open city until 30th June. But now that the armistice had been signed and France divided into occupied and unoccupied zones, Bordeaux found itself in the occupied sector. It was therefore no longer a fitting capital for what soon became known as the 'Vichy Government'.

It was a surprise to many that Admiral Darlan had joined this government. There was a particular and special quality about the blue-eyed Gascon and the way he organised the Navy's life. As he had done since the outbreak of war, Darlan contrived to keep himself and the French Admiralty aloof and apart. There were good reasons for this. The politicians of the Third Republic, with certain exceptions, were not held in great esteem, and the French High Command had hardly distinguished itself in the fall of France. Only the Navy retained its integrity.

The Navy had failed in no battles, it had lost no wars. With superb courage and seamanship it had got its two greatest and not fully completed battlecruisers, the *Jean Bart* and the *Richelieu* away from metropolitan France to the safety of Casablanca and Dakar. The French Navy remained a highly disciplined, competent and effective force. Indeed it had proved to be the only substantial bargaining counter in the recent armistice negotiations. It was Darlan's intention to keep it that way.

On the outbreak of war in the autumn of 1939, one of Darlan's first actions had been to remove the upper echelons of the French Admiralty fifty miles out of Paris to Maintenon. The formal reason for this had been given as the expected bombardment of Paris from the air. In fact it was both to avoid the politicians and to remove his staff from the distractions of Paris such as wives, mistresses and good living. When Captain Holland had been Naval Attaché at Maintenon, his wife had been allowed to come down and see him only on Sundays, the rest of the time she spent alone in the Paris apartment.

Now that the French Government thought of establishing itself in Vichy, Darlan determined to retain the Navy's aloofness by looking for suitable headquarters some little distance away. This decision – and the temporary interruption in communication which it caused – was to play an unexpected part in the tragedy about to begin.

'Why didn't the French Government go to North Africa and continue to fight from there? Alternatively, why don't Morocco and Algeria break away and act independently as General Mittelhauser wanted to do from Beirut in the Eastern Mediterranean?'

This was the sort of thing the Staff Officer (Intelligence) at Gibraltar was asked at briefing conferences and, although any answer he gave to such hypothetical questions would be largely guesswork, Commander Geoffrey Birley, R.N., was nevertheless the best informed man in the Western Mediterranean and his opinion, therefore, was valuable. Birley was on the staff of the Flag Officer, Gibraltar. Initially he was not put in the picture about Operation Catapult although, when his office was asked for up-to-date charts of swept channels at Oran (i.e. of safe routes through minefields), it did not take a genius to guess what might be about to happen.

Now as he looked out of his office in the Dockyard Tower at the great ships of Force H arriving in the shadow of the Rock, he thought back to his own last visit to Oran a few days before and on all that had been happening in his 'parish' since the fall of France. Birley had been holding down this Intelligence job since the beginning of 1939. Until the collapse of France his liaison with the French in North Africa had been excellent. Even now, when direct communications had been severed, the daily ferry to the international port of Tangier still operated and Tangier was one of the great collecting and interchange markets for intelligence en route to London, Berlin and other interested capitals.

There was, indeed, no dearth of the raw material of intelligence. It was part of Birley's job to sift and collate the facts and opinions which daily coursed through his office and to be able to present to his Admiral and to the Director of Naval Intelligence at the Admiralty a coherent picture of the local scene on which decisions could be made.

This was Sunday, 30th June, and a week previously he and his Admiral, Sir Dudley Burton Napier North, K.C.V.O., C.B., C.S.I., C.M.G., A.D.C., Naval Aide-de-Camp and Extra Equerry to the King and previously the Vice-Admiral Commanding H.M. Yachts, who had taken passage to Oran in the destroyer *Douglas* together with *Capitaine de Frégate* de Bryson, the French Naval Liaison Officer then attached to his staff. The armistice terms had just become known and the British Admiralty had required North to sound out Admiral Estéva, the Commander-in-Chief of the French Naval Forces (other than the *Flotte de Raid*) in North Africa, on the possibility of joining up with the British. But Estéva was away to the east at Bizerta and although an aircraft could have got him to Oran in a few short hours, he chose not to be available. In consequence Dudley North and his party had to be content with a meeting in Oran with Admiral Gensoul, the C.-in-C. of the French Atlantic Fleet, and Admiral Jarry, the Admiral Commanding Oran and Mers-el-Kebir. It was not a propitious start.

HMS *Douglas* arrived in Oran around noon. 'Keep an eye on what ships are in harbour,' North had told his Staff Officer (Intelligence) 'and also check on the height of the breakwater.' To a trained mind this looked like a presage of things to come and was perhaps the easiest task Birley was given since it entailed no movement. Birley was suffering from a carbuncle on his thigh the size of an ashtray but, if he was in physical pain, it was nothing compared to the emotional state of the French Admirals they had come to meet.

Jarry, who had a long grey beard 'down to his navel', was weeping unashamedly like a child and Gensoul, a large and imposing man, was also in tears. It was not a day for Dudley North's usual approach to negotiations of this kind which tended to be sophisticated and laced with champagne. Gensoul told them he had been planning to bombard Genoa the following day but all operations had had to be abandoned and they were 'waiting on instructions from Darlan'.

This was the definitive statement and the British visitors could get nothing further from men so clearly in a state of shock. They set off back to Gibraltar at 1600 hours and at midnight the armistice between France and Germany came into force. Admiral Gensoul's report on this visit, made to the investigating tribunal after the war, gives a slightly different account: 'On a date I cannot exactly specify – end of June, perhaps, or 1st July, I received on board the *Dunkerque* at Mers-el-Kebir the visit of the English Admiral Dudley North commanding the base at Gibraltar who had come to talk to me in a friendly way about the general situation. He seemed a little disturbed at the situation of his forces and I had the impression that he was unaware of the imminent arrival in the Mediterranean of Admiral Somerville's Fleet [this was absolutely true since Force H did not then exist]. He made me no proposition of any sort. I think he came to find out our state of morale which was *nettement anglophile*. I confirmed to him that in no case whatever would our ships fall into German or Italian hands.'

The *état d'esprit nettement anglophile* was to take a severe beating in ten days' time.

Across to the west, things were no better at Casablanca. The auxiliary cruiser *Massiglia* had arrived there on 24th June together with what Churchill called 'its unlucky band of patriots'. The voyage from Bordeaux had begun with a mutiny, since the crew looked on their distinguished passengers as rats on the run from danger, and was to end in paralysis and, for some of the passengers, in prison.

Georges Mandel, who had earlier said that if he had not been Jewish he would have seized the reins of government, was the leader of a group of French Senators and Deputies which included Daladier and Campinchi, the Minister of Marine. They intended to set up a Resistance administration in North Africa and continue the fight. From this group of people Darlan was conspicuously absent. Possibly he saw their departure from the centre of power as a convenience to himself.

At all events the Proclamation to the World written by Mandel and entrusted to the Havas Agency got no further than Governor-General Noguès, who stopped its dissemination and instead sent it on to Darlan and Pétain. This action resulted in Mandel's arrest and in his being held *incommunicado* on board the *Massiglia*. Such was the state of affairs when Mr Duff Cooper, the British Minister of Information, and Lord Gort, who was about to be Governor of Gibraltar, arrived in a Sunderland flying boat on 26th June on the personal orders of

Churchill to try to contact any French politicians with the will to resist. This mission was to be an utter failure.

The Governor-General avoided his uninvited British guests. The Deputy Governor, Morice, said he had no option but to obey the orders of his superiors. Mandel and his *confrères* were being treated as escaped prisoners, which was certainly not their status on leaving Bordeaux, and were expressly forbidden contact with the outside world. So the British party morosely returned in their flying boat to the United Kingdom and that was the end of that. Mandel was later handed over to the Germans by the Vichy Government and murdered in the forest of Fontainebleau in 1944.

The only conclusion sadly drawn by Intelligence from these two separate visits was that the colonial French who controlled north and west Africa were obstinate, negative, touchy and frightened. The spirit amongst their younger subordinates may well have been different but there was no practical way of finding this out, and until they were over the cataclysmic shock of their country's defeat no expression of any will to continue the fight would be detected.

Chapter 3

Force H was to be a mere forty-eight hours in Gibraltar. Pressure on everyone was steadily and increasingly applied. Amongst the few who were aware of the facts – fully aware of the facts – tension became almost unbearable.

On Sunday evening, 30th June, just fifty hours after leaving Portsmouth, HMS *Arethusa* berthed alongside in Gibraltar. Almost before 'Finished with Engines' was rung down, Somerville set about transferring his flag to HMS *Hood*. Although junior to Sir Dudley North, the Flag Officer North Atlantic Station, whose base was Gibraltar, Somerville had been made Senior Officer of a seagoing fleet and had the status of a Commander-in-Chief.

This status had been established almost accidentally in the hurly-burly of the previous Thursday whilst ferreting out a staff from the Admiralty. Keith Walter, his Flag Lieutenant and Signal Officer to be, who had previously served with Somerville as a Midshipman, found himself in his own words 'footling about in the Signals Division of the Admiralty on the early development of radar' when he was suddenly sent for by the newly appointed Senior Officer, Force H.

'I've been landed with you as my Signal Officer and Flag Lieutenant, God help me,' Somerville had said with a smile, and had immediately put him to work to find such essential ratings as an Admiral's coxswain out of a Portsmouth Barracks long denuded of skilled personnel. That was one problem. Another was to ensure that Most Secret communication (the phrase Top Secret came in with the Americans) between the Admiralty and the new C.-in-C. would be possible.

For this purpose special reciphering tables were necessary so that messages intended only for the eyes of the Commander-in-Chief could not be read by lesser mortals. It was thus for communication purposes that the Flag Officer, Force H became one of the élite and Keith Walter walked about for the rest of that day with the necessary reciphering tables in his hand.

This new Fleet appointment was something of an affront for the Flag Officer, Gibraltar and the Vice-Admiral, Aircraft Carriers, both of whom had run things in their own way locally up till then. But from the moment Force H arrived at the Rock, the black task ahead of them dictated its own pace. This pace and the gravity of what was about to be done put the petty jealousies of command out of everyone's thoughts.

Immediately they arrived, Somerville and his Flag Lieutenant went to call on Sir Dudley North at the Mount, the Flag Officer, Gibraltar's 18th century residence half-way up the Rock.

'Operation Catapult?' North said when he had read the Admiralty orders Somerville showed him, 'Boomerang would be a more appropriate word! This puts us all at risk.'

On the spot service opposition to the operation thus began. It voiced itself in different ways depending upon the status and responsibility of the objector but a common note of disgust and horror at what was proposed made itself felt at once. Commander G. K. Collett, R.N., who had lately been British Naval Liaison Officer with the French Atlantic Fleet, had returned to London but there were two other ex-liaison officers, Lieutenant Commanders Davies and Spearman, who were still at Gibraltar. The former, a submarine officer, had been on the staff of the French Admiral (Submarines) at Bizerta. Spearman had served on Admiral Estéva's staff at Algiers. Both protested vehemently that under no circumstances should force be used.

'French senior officers are exhausted. They are bewildered old men. They are understaffed. They withdraw very easily into their shells. But they are still full of pride and prickly about the honour of France. Certainly,' they went on, 'we should make our proposals known to the more junior officers and men, if we can. These have been left very much to their own devices with neither reliable news nor a definite policy to work to. They moon about like lost sheep. Give them a firm and friendly lead and their influence might just have some feed-back effect on Admirals Estéva and Gensoul. Over there, only those officers in close touch with the high command know what is going on or what is being done in their name.'

Admiral North expressed his opinion somewhat differently. 'Winnie must be mad,' he said in his quiet and gentle voice. 'I see what he's after but this is a bloody silly way of going about it. Why not send me a decent yacht, let me fill it up with champagne and pretty Wrens, and I'll sail in and get the French myself.' Not, in the circumstances, a very practical suggestion but then North, as a late Vice-Admiral Commanding H.M. Yachts, was strong on the political and social expediencies of naval life. Tragically, there was no time for finesse in a situation where finesse was to be of supreme importance.

It was not only at Gibraltar that opposition to 'Catapult' expressed itself. That same Sunday morning from the other end of the Mediterranean, Vice-Admiral Sir Andrew Browne Cunningham, the Commander-in-Chief, Mediterranean, had signalled the Admiralty at 1105 objecting in the strongest terms to the proposal that French ships at Alexandria should be forcibly seized. He also told Their Lordships that the use of force at Oran might, in his opinion, have 'serious repercussions'. Somerville had intercepted this message an hour and a half before getting into Gib.

The serious repercussions were likely to fall first and foremost on Gibraltar itself. During the previous night the Admiralty had instructed Admiral North, 'to investigate the action which could be taken by Force H to neutralise bombardment in the event of Spain becoming hostile'.

'I was somewhat surprised at receiving this message,' Somerville wrote in his operation report, 'since I understood that a number of appreciations of the situation referred to had invariably reached the same conclusion, namely that Gibraltar as a naval base would immediately become untenable except, perhaps, for a few small craft and possibly submarines.'

North put it even more strongly, stating that: 'since the Germans would be co-operating actively with the Spaniards, it was idle to suppose that Gibraltar could be used as a naval base. Engagement of shore batteries by ships and *Ark Royal*'s aircraft could only silence some of the batteries temporarily.'

But what could they do? They expressed, freely amongst themselves and guardedly to the Admiralty, their acute distaste for the operation they had been ordered to execute. Any further objection would have been mutinous. The decision had been taken by the British War Cabinet and no option was left to the men on the spot but to carry out the orders they had been given.

So the forty-eight hours at Gibraltar came to an end.

Chapter 4

Force H left Gibraltar on the evening of 2nd July 1940. It was a fine sunny evening and there was no chance whatever of their departure passing unnoticed by the Spanish, German and Italian observers ensconced in Algeciras. Later, when Force H had to run vital convoys through to Malta, deception would be employed. The Fleet would leave at night. Then they would stealthily head west into the Atlantic as if to search out the German pocket-battleships preying on the various convoys to England from Africa and the Far East. A little later, in the darkest hours of the night, they would double back into the Mediterranean between the Pillars of Hercules, hoping not to be observed by Spanish or Moroccan fishing boats whose rewards for such information were considerable.

Now, however, it was different. 'By 1700,' Admiral Somerville's Report of Proceedings was to read, 'Force H had cleared the harbour and course was shaped to the eastward at 17 knots using screening diagram 7A and zigzag No. 10, until 2130, when the zigzag was stopped and speed reduced to 15 knots.'

They sailed with expectation on the lower deck and a sombre brooding, laced with the gravest misgiving, among the senior officers who knew the real purpose of the mission. The prospect was indeed grim. 'You are charged', Churchill signalled towards midnight, 'with one of the most disagreeable and difficult tasks that a British Admiral has ever been faced with, but we have complete confidence in you and rely on you to carry it out relentlessly.'

This was of small consolation to Somerville, a few days before his 58th birthday and for the first time in command of a powerful seagoing fleet in war. He stood now on the Admiral's bridge of HMS *Hood* staring out into the Mediterranean night. He had undertaken this 'hard and thankless' job at the shortest notice. His advice had been ignored. Never before had he embarked on a mission with greater reluctance and, in his opinion, with less real chance of success. The next day would undoubtedly be a nightmare. Both he and his Secretary, who had just deciphered the Admiralty signal and who now stood beside him on the darkened bridge, knew the realities of what lay immediately ahead of them all.

'When are we detaching *Foxhound*?' the Admiral asked his Chief of Staff who was standing near him on the bridge.

'At 0400, sir. She should be in visual touch with the Mers-el-Kebir Port War Signal Station at about 0630.'

Below them the 42,000 tons of HMS *Hood*, at that time the most powerful warship in the world, stretched out before them in the calm Mediterranean darkness. Her turrets of huge 15-inch guns were trained fore and aft, her ship's company, except for the duty watch, were turned in, their hammocks swaying gently along the messdecks. 'Action Stations' would not be sounded off, barring emergencies, until shortly before the Fleet arrived in the vicinity of Oran.

To Bill Farrell, the Admiral's Secretary, the overnight passage to the North African coast represented the only breathing space he had enjoyed since leaving London five days ago. Tomorrow they would see the results of their labours. Tomorrow a firm and definite answer would be had to the demands they were ordered to make.

Now, however, as he stood beside his Admiral whom he had only met for the first time under a week ago, the pressure of events and the hard work they had all had to do slipped into the background of his mind. The magnificence of being at sea in the 'Mighty *Hood*', the almost schoolboyish thrill of peering out into the darkness and seeing the two 30,000-ton battleships *Valiant* and *Resolution*, the flat-topped aircraft carrier *Ark Royal*, the two cruisers *Arethusa* and *Enterprise* and the eleven sprightly destroyers protecting the battle fleet from enemy submarines, reminded him vividly of first principles, of why he had joined the Navy at all, of what it was all about in this initial year of the war.

The relationship between any Commander-in-Chief and his staff, and especially his Secretary, is crucial to the success or otherwise of the Fleet he runs. The almost absolute power wielded by an Admiral in command of a seagoing force is tempered, intelligently or otherwise, by the way the staff interpret his decisions. They know – or they hope to be able to produce – the answers required.

The Secretary above all is privy to each and every secret the Admiral alone should know. Farrell, whose round-headed impassiveness concealed a sensitive and watchful intelligence, had not yet found himself completely at ease in this unexpected appointment. Everything was new. Ten days ago, as a junior Paymaster Lieutenant Commander, R.N., he had found himself somewhat improbably as the only R.N. officer in Jersey. There he had had to keep open the airport as a Channel Island staging post for R.A.F. Bombers needing to refuel *en route* to or from Northern Italian targets. He had gone there in a rush and he had got out again in a rush, evacuating his tiny outfit shortly before the Germans arrived.

Farrell had never been an Admiral's Secretary before. Now he was faced with the personal management of a man who was to become one of the most brilliant Admirals of the war, a man of drive, impatience, humour and charm, fresh from the rigours of Dunkirk, crisp in behaviour with an underlying kindliness but not apt to suffer fools gladly.

The calm passage east was now interrupted by a priority signal flashed back by the Captain (Destroyers). 'Torpedo exploded ahead of HMS *Vortigern* in position C. Am detaching *Vortigern* and *Vidette* to hunt U boat' – an unsuccessful search which took up the next 65 minutes. By this time Force H was a good fifteen sea miles nearer its destination.

This was the only incident of record in the approach to Mers-el-Kebir and as the short Mediterranean night wore on, those who would be under especial strain the following day went below to their cabins or their hammocks to get a little sleep.

Shortly before 0200 an Admiralty message was deciphered stating that, although no time limit was set for acceptance of the British demands, it was very important that the operation should be completed during the daylight hours of 3rd July.

To Winston Churchill, to the First Sea Lord and to the other 'night watchers' in London, this timing was, indeed, of the utmost importance. They alone saw the picture whole. They alone knew what else was under way in other parts of the world so far as the French Fleet was concerned. It was going to be a crucially delicate twenty-four hours.

Plans of the highest secrecy had been made and were at that moment being put into effect, by which those units of the French Navy, then in British ports, would be commandeered by the British, it was hoped without loss of blood. This was an involved and tricky decision to take and an even more dangerous one to execute. But what were the alternatives?

At this moment there was but one major obstacle to Hitler's almost certain victory and that was Churchill's relentless will.

As it turned out, the United States of America were almost eighteen months away from active participation. Except for the 25 fighter squadrons which the War Cabinet had refused to send to France, the United Kingdom stood virtually defenceless. Even the retention of those last few squadrons, obstinately insisted upon by Churchill, had cost the British an incalculable amount of French goodwill prior to the armistice.

Ahead lay possible invasion and the certain but unpredictable Battle of Britain. Only the Navy remained invincible. The Royal Navy of 1940 was, perhaps, the most powerful, flexible and sophisticated weapon Great Britain had ever possessed. But it could not be everywhere at once. Moreover, the balance of power, especially in the Mediterranean, had now been seriously disturbed.

With the French Navy on our side, the Italian Fleet had so far scarcely dared to leave harbour. But now that the French had suddenly disappeared from the political scene, their two great battlecruisers at Oran – the *Dunkerque* and the *Strasbourg* – could no longer be set against the Italian 'Fleet in being'.* Moreover, if the *Jean Bart* and the *Richelieu* could be seized at Casablanca and Dakar, then the odds would change dramatically against the British, who now faced the Germans alone. It was this simple but inevitable equation which, in essence, was the reason for the operation.

That night another naval officer in London was having a restless time. This was George Collett, the ex-liaison officer to the French Atlantic Fleet. Collett was a Commander of some six months' seniority and had now been attached as Liaison Officer to the newly appointed Admiral Commanding the Free French Naval Forces, an organisation which itself had only existed for two or three days.

Collett knew that Force H would now be forging steadily on towards Mers-el-Kebir and he thought back to the reverse journey he had made himself only a few days before. From February to June Collett had served on board the *Dunkerque*, the flagship of Admiral Gensoul, Commander-in-Chief of the French Atlantic Fleet. It had been an unusual and fascinating appointment. Then, after the armistice, Gensoul had put him on board a destroyer for Gibraltar and that had been the end of that.

On his return home he had reported to the Prime Minister and the First Sea Lord.

'What will the French Fleet do if they are offered these alternatives?' the First Sea Lord had asked him, showing him part of the draft ultimatum about to be presented. He had not been asked how the French would react to the threat of force.

'They will never allow their ships to fall into enemy hands,' Collett had answered, remembering the wardroom of the great French battleship with its outsize map of France on the bulk-

* A 'Fleet in being' could be defined as a naval force of capital ships ready and poised for action thus constituting a threat.

head. For the last six weeks of his stay on board the *Dunkerque* each daily advance of the German army had been marked up on this map.

Describing this to the Staff Officer (Intelligence) in Gibraltar, Collett had said:

'It was tragic to see the reaction as each chap's home got overrun. The *Dunkerque* has the pick of the French Navy on board. As you know, the French only have one real Fleet existing as an entity on its own and the *Flotte de l'Atlantique* is very conscious of being *la crême de la crême*. Every officer and man on board the Flagship has been handpicked. They come from all parts of France, though perhaps mainly from the Brest and Toulon areas. Thus, as the German advance went on, there was no one who was not affected in some way or other. Anxiety about their homes and families in metropolitan France is the big factor which must be continuously borne in mind when assessing the morale of the French Navy in general and the Atlantic Fleet in particular.'

That night as French warships in Plymouth and Portsmouth were to be stealthily – 'perfidiously' – seized by the Royal Navy, as Force H drew near Oran for its tough and unpredictable assignment, with Admiral Godfroy's Force X providing tomorrow's headache for the British Commander-in-Chief at Alexandria, George Collett thought back over his months in the *Dunkerque* and tried to imagine how the French would react to what was about to happen. It was not going to be easy to walk into the Free French Admiral's office the next morning with a cheerful '*Bonjour*' on the lips.

In Mers-el-Kebir itself all was quiet but a shrewd observer would have seen this calm as the numbness of shock and despair. Now that defeat had generally to be accepted, a new way of life was going to have to be found. The officers and men of the four great battleships moored with their sterns to the mole, of the six Fleet destroyers anchored across the harbour, and of the venerable seaplane carrier *Commandant Teste* were all in different ways suffering from the aftermath of crisis. Now that the war was over for France, what was to happen to them all? What was demobilisation going to mean in fact? How long were the British going to hold out alone?

As with trained fighting men the world over, the standard reaction to an unknown situation was to fall back on discipline and routine. Like any piece of clockwork, naval life is made up of interconnecting wheels which must all work together if the mechanism is to move. So while the demobilisation of reservists who came from North Africa had already begun, it was necessary to keep those who remained as fully occupied as possible.

On board the 26,000-ton battleship *Dunkerque* daily activities continued in the way they had done since the ship commissioned. The 55 officers of wardroom rank and the 23 who comprised the staff of the Commander-in-Chief exchanged the usual courtesies but kept much to themselves as they always did. They shook hands with each other in the French manner first thing in the morning and last thing at night. They tended to treat each other with slightly more formality than their British counterparts would have done (Collett found that his right hand was exhausted from *le shake-hand* before even sitting down to breakfast), in the forenoon they drank double Muscadets instead of pink gin, when ashore in Oran they had less of a puritan guilt complex about the local attractions than their Anglo-Saxon opposite numbers. Otherwise they were the same highly specialised officers and men doing something for which there was now no longer any requirement.

The Executive Officer of the *Dunkerque, Capitaine de Frégate* Pierre Tanguy, nicknamed 'le grand Pierre' or 'Tanguy-Tanguy', because of his habit of repeating everything, looked back on the daily orders he had issued for the 24 hours just ending and authorised the *feuille de service* for the third of July. The Starboard Watch would be on duty. The usual routine of scrubbing deck, cleaning quarters and physical training would take place in the hot North African day. The Duty boats were listed and the times for shore leave and bathing parties set down. The previous day there had been a Roman Catholic Mass *pour les morts de la guerre* (their Commander-in-Chief was a Protestant), tomorrow a diving party consisting of a Petty Officer and five men would join *Le Prieur* for training. Rangefinding and other specialist exercises would take place. The usual shore patrols would be landed and the times the Marsa cinema operated (*prix des places 2 Fr*) were listed. At 0730 the *Dunkerque* would play the *Terrible* at Basket-ball and at 1600 the Fleet Water Polo championship would see the *Dunkerque* taking on the *Commandant Teste*, provision being made along the mole for 50 spectators amongst whom members of the second team were directed to be present. In other words there was nothing out of the ordinary in the daily orders which would be read and noted by the 1,431 officers and men of the flagship of the French Atlantic Fleet. All was calm and quiet and the recent terrible events on the continent of Europe a million miles away.

Towards midnight *Lieutenant de Vaisseau* Bernard Dufay, the tall, thin *Aide-de-Camp*, a post in the French Navy which combines the duties of Admiral's Secretary and Flag Lieutenant, decoded the situation report from the French Admiralty. This was shorter than usual, both because there was little to say and because the French Admiralty was in process of moving from its temporary headquarters at Nérac, south-east of Bordeaux, to Vichy in central France. Since there was nothing of urgency to report and Admiral Gensoul had already turned in, Dufay decided to do likewise. There was no indication that the day which was about to break on the fortified harbour of Mers-el-Kebir would, in a few short hours, *bouleverser* the French Atlantic Fleet and those who served in it, let alone have repercussions upon the whole future progress of the war.

On board the destroyer HMS *Foxhound* the man who was to bear the brunt of the coming negotiations climbed up on the bridge to have a final look round and say good-night to Commander Peters, the ship's Commanding Officer. Captain Cedric Holland, R.N., was taking passage in the destroyer and 'Farmer' Peters had given his distinguished guest the use of his main cabin aft under the quarterdeck. Up top it continued to be a fine cloudless night.

'She's still there, sir, safe and sound,' Peters said pointing at the great lump of the *Ark Royal* looming astern of them on the starboard quarter.

'Keep an eye on her for me,' Holland said, 'I'm going to turn in for a while. Call me at 0600 if I haven't shown up before.'

Then lowering his tall, slightly angular frame off the bridge, 'Hooky' Holland went down aft to turn in. Holland, almost inevitably nicknamed Hooky not only because of his nose but also because of the 'Hook of —' was currently Captain of HMS *Ark Royal*. But because of his recent appointment as British Naval Attaché in Paris, because he spoke the language fluently and had both a liking and an understanding of the French, he had temporarily handed over command of the Navy's most famous aircraft carrier in order personally to explain the British Government's ultimatum to the French Commander-in-Chief.

He had accepted this daunting task with the gravest misgiving. Indeed, before leaving Gibraltar, he had spent an agonising forenoon composing a formal letter to the Flag Officer, Force H, which would unquestionably have resulted in a court-martial, setting out his strong objections to Operation Catapult and asking to be relieved of his command.

But the letter was never sent. 'Orders are orders' is perhaps the quickest way of explaining why. However disgusted he was by the brutal perspective ahead, thirty years of naval training and responsibility cannot lightly be set aside. He was a man put under authority having under him others and, like the Centurion at Capernaum, he understood the meaning of discipline. Thus with a heavy heart and an almost paralysing reluctance, he was now about to carry out the mission for which Their Lordships thought him especially suited.

Back in his cabin, Holland tried to order his thoughts before going to sleep. He reread the signal Somerville had sent him just before eight o'clock that evening saying that according to Commander Collett, whom Holland remembered as Liaison Officer to Admiral Gensoul, the French had a plan to demilitarise their ships in Mers-el-Kebir at short notice. 'If you are satisfied with this scheme, the best course might be to put it into force' – a somewhat easier statement to make than to effect.

Wryly and for the umpteenth time since orders had been received, he began to read through the two definitive signals the Admiralty had sent to the Flag Officer, Force H the previous night. Somewhere in these signals he hoped to find encouragement and perhaps a glint of hope. But once more, as he read them through, his heart began to sink.

He put down the first signal and thought. There was very little margin to manoeuvre. Beneath him the destroyer's screws threshed the ship nearer and nearer the point of decision. He tried to remember the sort of man Gensoul had appeared on the few occasions he had met him after taking up his appointment as Naval Attaché in Paris two and a half years ago.

He knew what he looked like. Physically the French Admiral was a tall, somewhat ponderous man of around sixty. Admiral Gensoul had always struck him as reserved but, in fact, Holland knew very little else about him. Certainly he was no Darlan, the brilliant 'political Admiral' who had regenerated the French Navy virtually from scratch, who was its only Admiral of the Fleet and who was generally and rightly revered.

Holland suspected that Gensoul was where he was because of 'Buggins' turn next'. French senior naval officers were usually older than their British counterparts because the opportunities of significant command were fewer. Gensoul, he knew, had been Commander-in-Chief of the Atlantic Fleet or *La Flotte de Raid* since 1938. For a brief time the previous winter he had actually had HMS *Hood* under his operational command.

He knew Gensoul to be fourth in succession to the throne, so to speak. In other words if Darlan were to find himself unable to operate freely, command of the Navy would pass first to Admiral de Laborde, late of Brest, then to Admiral Estéva at Algiers, next to Admiral Abrial who had been the French Admiral in charge of Dunkirk and then finally to Admiral Gensoul. But would Gensoul feel able to make the fundamental decision which would be asked of him tomorrow?

He picked up the copy he had been given of the second Admiralty Most Secret and Immediate cipher to the Flag Officer, Force H. This bore a time of origin five minutes after the first one but had not been received in *Hood* at Gibraltar till just after six that morning.

'Following is the communication to be made to the French Admiral at Oran referred to in my 0103/2nd July' the signal began,

'1. H.M. Government have sent me to inform you as follows:

'2. They agreed to French Government approaching the German Government only on condition that if an armistice was concluded the French Fleet should be sent to British ports to prevent it falling into hands of the enemy. The Council of Ministers declared on 18th June that before capitulating on land, the French Fleet would join up with the British Force or sink itself.'

This error of fact was not to be established until later and was certainly not then known at the level of a seagoing fleet. If the above had been taken as the basis of British Admiralty thinking, Captain Holland *en route* to Oran had no cause whatever to doubt it. Moreover, it made sense. He knew that France and England had signed a treaty in the spring of 1940, just before the German blitzkrieg but after six months of the *drôle de guerre*, by which both countries bound themselves not to make a separate peace. He continued with his reading:

'3. Whilst the present French Government may consider that terms of their armistice with Germany and Italy are reconcilable with these undertakings, H.M. Government finds it impossible from their previous experience to believe Germany and Italy will not at any moment which suits them seize French warships and use them against Britain and her allies. Italian armistice prescribes that French ships should return to metropolitan ports and under armistice France is required to yield up units for coast defence and minesweeping.'

This, too, was plain common sense. Whatever 'solemn pledges' and 'words of honour' might be proffered by Hitler, distrust of the Germans went very deep in Anglo-Saxon thinking. The

Great War had begun with the invasion of Belgium contrary to a treaty 'torn up as a scrap of paper'. Events in Austria and Czechoslovakia in 1938 and 1939 had done nothing to increase respect for the German word of honour. Therefore the belief set out above had a very practical basis.

'4. It is impossible for us, your comrades up till now, to allow your fine ships to fall into the power of German or Italian enemy. We are determined to fight on until the end, and if we win as we think we shall, we shall never forget that France was our ally, that our interests are the same as yours and that our common enemy is Germany. Should we conquer, we solemnly declare that we shall restore the greatness and territory of France. For this purpose we must be sure that the best ships of the French Navy will also not be used against us by the common foe.'

So far so good. Fine sentiments had been expressed and very little exception could be taken to the message up to this point despite the implication that 'the present French Government' had behaved with questionable faith. Now, however, the steel began to show through.

'5. In these circumstances, H.M. Government have instructed me to demand the French Fleet now at Mers-el-Kebir and Oran shall act in accordance with one of the following alternatives:

(a) Sail with us and continue to fight for victory against the the Germans and Italians.

(b) Sail with reduced crews under our control to a British port. The reduced crews will be repatriated at the earliest moment.

If either of these courses is adopted by you we will restore your ships to France at the conclusion of the war, or pay full compensation if they are damaged meanwhile.

(c) Alternatively if you feel bound to stipulate that your ships should not be used against Germans or Italians, since this would break the armistice, then sail them with us with reduced crews to some French port in the West Indies – Martinique, for instance – where they can be demilitarised to our satisfaction or perhaps be entrusted to the United States of America and remain safely until the end of the war, the crews being repatriated.'

Once again he paused in his reading trying to visualise the effect this would have on the French Commander-in-Chief. His intention the next day was not to show this document to Gensoul until he had conveyed the gist of the proposals verbally in French. He had dealt with many similarly delicate matters in this way during his stint as Naval Attaché. Here his background gave him a detachment, possibly even an aloofness which was of use, although like others in his mould, he knew instinctively when to unbend and apply a little charm were this likely to oil the wheels.

He had good reason to think in such a way. Should the final paragraph of the Admiralty signal be shown to the French C.-in-C. before he had had time to absorb and consider the foregoing implications, the French sense of honour and pride, which had taken such a hammering in the last few weeks, would immediately obstruct understanding and progress. Thus the inevitable threat – on which it all depended – must be kept hidden until the very last when all else had failed, as indeed it had been so placed in the signal itself.

'If you refuse these fair offers,' the Admiralty instructed him in the end to say, 'I must with profound regret require you to sink your ships within six hours. Finally, failing the above, I have the orders of His Majesty's Government to use whatever force may be necessary to prevent your ships from falling into German or Italian hands.'

Well, there it was. That was the gravamen, to use one of Churchill's words, of the coming day. He put the documents back in his briefcase and lay down in the gently rolling destroyer cabin for a few hours' uneasy rest. No one slept deeply or well these days, least of all with the responsibilities Holland carried on his shoulders and which were so soon to be discharged.

As HMS *Foxhound* detached from Force H and increased speed in order to arrive at the time ordered, the operation of taking possession of French warships in British home ports had begun. Hundreds of French Officers and men had been hustled

71

ashore in their night attire and a British submarine officer and a Leading Seaman had already been shot dead in the *Surcouf*, the world's largest submarine. In Berlin, Hitler that same night gave his service chiefs the executive order to plan the invasion of Britain. In the harbours of Mers-el-Kebir and Oran the French Atlantic Fleet lay quietly at anchor, as the cool light of dawn began slowly to suffuse from the east.

Chapter 5

Thus in the early morning of Wednesday, 3rd July, HMS *Foxhound* approached the fortified harbour of Mers-el-Kebir, and at 0545 local time, which was an hour ahead of Greenwich Mean Time, she attempted to raise the French Port War Signal Station. There appeared to be little sign of life.

It was a fine day and the gentle dawn mist which hazes over the Mediterranean at this time of year had already begun to lift from the flat, almost lake-like calm of the sea. Facing the 1350-ton British destroyer, as she nosed quietly towards the harbour entrance, stood the stark, dun-coloured hills encircling Mers-el-Kebir. Sandy, treeless and arid, the bareness of these foothills, which were to form the décor to the day, brought to mind the vast empty Sahara stretching away south beyond the Atlas mountains.

The timelessness of the scene was almost symbolic. Only the masts and upperworks of the great French ships reminded them of the realities of the moment. It was going to be very hot.

Although HMS *Foxhound* was closed up at Action Stations, she bore no outwardly belligerent signs. Her four 4·7 inch guns were trained fore and aft and on deck the ordinary number of personnel necessary to bring the ship into port and to anchor her were standing by in the usual way.

On the destroyer bridge, in addition to the navigating party, stood the ship's captain, Commander G. H. Peters, R.N., a typical John Bull with powerful rounded shoulders and pronounced features, the spare ascetic-looking Captain Holland and the two other ex-liaison officers, Lieutenant Commanders Spearman and Davies. All were keyed up and tense. This was

73

in direct contrast with the atmosphere of early morning tranquillity suggested by the French Fleet in harbour as it lay there waiting for the normal day's activities to begin.

It took nearly a quarter of an hour to get an answer from the Port War Signal Station. At 0558 permission was requested to enter the port. No immediate reaction to this was visible and *Foxhound* continued slowly under way as the sun rose and the daylight broadened. Thirty-five minutes after they had first called up the Mers-el-Kebir signal station, a similar message requesting permission to enter was passed to the Admiral Superintendent of Oran, together with a brief statement to the effect that the British Admiralty was sending Captain Holland to confer with Admiral Gensoul. Both signals were flashed in morse by Aldis lamp in the normal way from the bridge of the destroyer. Both messages were in French. Receipt was acknowledged but otherwise nothing happened. The long wait had begun.

Meanwhile reveillé had sounded on board the French ships and the day's routine got under way as it does in every warship all over the world. The 'housekeeping' jobs of washing the decks and of generally cleaning ship started up, accompanied by the bugle calls and pipes which in naval life cause things to happen. At 0630 on board the flagship *Dunkerque* three sections of the shoregoing party in grey rig were mustered and at 0700 this party went down the gangways into three of the ship's boats and set off for the landward side of the harbour.

At this time there was still no sign of the approaching British Fleet. Radar was then in its infancy and the French did not have it at all. The horizon, therefore, remained, as it had done since the beginning of time, the end of the visible world. Beyond what the eye could see, anything or nothing could be happening. Until shortly after 0900, when Force H hove in sight, all that the French could observe was that one British destroyer had arrived off Oran and had asked permission to enter harbour.

But this apparently simple request did not strike Admiral Gensoul as innocuous. Now that the armistice with Germany and Italy had been signed, how was the approach of a British man-of-war, albeit a small one, to be regarded? What did the British want? Would the arrival of a British warship and communication with her be construed as an infringement of the armistice terms? Captain Holland had been 100 per cent right in one assessment of the French Commander-in-Chief – he was determined above all to be correct and to ensure that no action on his part could possibly endanger the French nation in this dark period it was about to enter. Hence the initial delay and reluctance to meet.

Holland had foreseen this reaction. Before leaving Gibraltar, he had told Somerville that Gensoul 'might be at pains to conceal from his officers and men the alternatives proposed for acceptance'. It had therefore been decided to try to cut the ground from under his feet by broadcasting the terms *en clair* and in French, hoping that the younger officers and men could at least bring pressure to bear on the French Admiral and at worst would at least know what it was all about. This was ingenuous but possibly worth a try.

At 0709, therefore, when after over an hour's waiting no permission to enter harbour had yet been received and two hours before the main British Fleet appeared, Holland sent a prepared signal to Gensoul taking care that every French ship in port would also receive the message.

'The British Admiralty has sent Captain Holland to confer with you. The Royal Navy hopes that their proposals will enable you and the valiant and glorious French Navy to be by our side. In these circumstances your ships would remain yours and no one need have anxiety for the future. The British Fleet is at sea off Oran waiting to welcome you.'

Permission for *Foxhound* to enter harbour was received at 0742, very nearly two hours after first being requested. Ten minutes later a pilot came aboard bringing instructions for the British destroyer to proceed inside Mers-el-Kebir and to berth near the *Dunkerque*.

'I don't think that's a good idea,' Holland said to Peters, out of the hearing of the French pilot. 'Once inside the boom [the

75

line of nets which in those days protected any naval harbour from submarine or torpedo attack] we might easily be prevented from sailing if things go wrong. Anchor just outside the net and I'll go in in the motorboat.'

Accordingly at 0805 *Foxhound* anchored in a position 1·6 miles 115° from Mers-el-Kebir Light and a few minutes later the French Admiral's barge was seen to be approaching with Lieutenant Dufay, the French Flag Lieutenant, on board. Dufay was an old friend of Holland's and this augured well. Or so he ventured to hope.

For *Lieutenant de Vaisseau* Bernard Dufay, the most shattering twenty-four hours in his naval career had begun quietly enough. Unlike the British Navy, a French Admiral's personal mess does not include his *Aide-de-Camp* but is confined to his Chief of Staff and Flag Captain. Dufay, therefore, was breakfasting in the wardroom of the *Dunkerque* when he was sent for by his Admiral.

In the ordinary course of events he would have gone along at about 0800 with the previous night's situation report which he had personally deciphered. Now something unusual must have happened. He entered the Admiral's cabin and found the Commander-in-Chief in conference with the Chief of Staff, *Capitaine de Vaisseau* Danbé. Both were obviously disturbed and irritated. It was 0745.

The Chief of Staff told him that the British Admiralty had sent Captain Holland in a destroyer to confer with Admiral Gensoul.

'You see how it is,' the Admiral commented. 'Last week they sent me Admiral North, today they send me a Captain. Next time it will be a Petty Officer.'

It was evident, right from the start, that questions of pride and honour were involved. Dufay was a regular officer in his early thirties. Like his opposite number on Admiral Somerville's staff he was in a special position, privy to all the secret information available and necessary to the functioning of the

Commander-in-Chief, for whom he had a high personal regard. If it is true that no man is a hero to his valet, it must also be clear that no man can exercise the high responsibilities of office without the loyal understanding of his close subordinates. Admiral Gensoul undoubtedly had this in full measure from his tall, thin and quick-brained secretary-cum-flag lieutenant.

Dufay had become Gensoul's A.D.C. almost by accident (much as Somerville had had to pick his staff without the peacetime leisure and freedom of choice) but he gave his somewhat austere and *renfermé* Admiral not only the full co-operation called for by ordinary regulations but also the leavening of wit. Dufay was *intelligent* in the French meaning of the word. Every Admiral's Secretary and Flag Lieutenant needs perforce to be something of an interpreter even in his own language. Dufay possessed these qualities and in addition spoke English with a reasonable fluency. Now he studied his Admiral and also the Chief of Staff, whom he privately regarded as something of a 'Yes man'.

'At least it is Captain Holland they've sent,' he ventured. He had come to know and respect the one-time British Naval Attaché on the previous visits Captain Holland had made to the Fleet from his headquarters at Paris and Maintenon. Whatever was about to happen, it was a help to have had previous experience of the personalities involved and to realise that Holland, in turn, knew Admiral Darlan personally and most of the high French officers on whom the fate of the Navy depended.

'The British have got a nerve,' the Chief of Staff remarked testily. 'They must surely realise that, in view of the armistice terms, this visit is highly improper. The Commander-in-Chief cannot possibly receive or enter into negotiations with the British.'

'What do they want?' Dufay asked.

'I don't know. But I can guess.'

A slight pause ensued.

'Take the Chief of Staff's barge,' Gensoul said to his A.D.C. 'Go and see Captain Holland on board the *Foxhound*. Present him with my compliments and tell him that, in accordance with instructions from the French Admiralty, British ships are not authorised to communicate with the shore, to shelter or to refuel in French ports. You should accept from Captain Holland any documents he may be carrying for the Commander-in-Chief. Should Captain Holland be charged with a verbal mission, tell him I am prepared to send the Chief of Staff on board his destroyer to hear what it is.'

'Yes sir,' Dufay said and left the Admiral's cabin, his thoughts in a turmoil but with a certain buoyant hope that matters could be adjusted and that he would be playing a useful role in a delicate affair of state. Thus minded he set off in the Chief of Staff's dark blue vedette at 0815, very much aware as he passed the great *Strasbourg* and the other battleships *Provence* and *Bretagne* that the ships in harbour were rapidly becoming alert to a possible new development in their lives.

At this moment Force H was still beyond the horizon and the watching French could see no obvious reason, certainly no sinister reason for a small British warship to visit a port filled with the capital ships of the French Atlantic Fleet.

One of the first French naval officers to catch sight of the British main force at large off Oran, was *Enseigne de Vaisseau* Maurice Putz, a 26-year-old Savoyard whose family had moved south from Lorraine after the Franco-Prussian war.

Putz, whose job on board the *Dunkerque* was 'Sécurité' which in the Royal Navy went under the name of Damage Control, had landed at 0700 with that section of the ship's company sent ashore for recreation and bathing. This was part of the normal everyday routine, but as he went down the gangway, Putz felt strangely reluctant to leave the ship.

Like his brother officers Putz suffered recurring anxiety about the fate of his family since the German invasion of France. Such worries were never far from his mind. One of his brothers had been in the Maginot line and another in all likelihood was dead or had been made a prisoner of war on the Franco-Belgian front. The previous night there had been another of those frustrating and inconclusive arguments in the mess as to what they should do. Ought the French Navy to continue the war as an entity or should they individually try and fight on as *francs-tireurs*? Now, as they blinked their way down to the jetty in the early morning sunlight, they were astonished to see a British destroyer anchored just outside the boom, its White Ensign barely moving in the breeze. Something unexpected was afoot.

Putz asked if the recreational party should perhaps be cancelled but was told to carry on as ordered. Accordingly he marched about a fifth of the ship's company of *Dunkerque* the three to five kilometres up and around Fort de Santon to the bathing beach. There they did physical exercises and went swimming. But this morning such activity seemed irksome and pointless. It was all such a waste of time. They were due back on board at 1045 but a sense of restless impatience drove them to set off on the return journey earlier than ordered. The recreational area they used was on the far side of Fort Santon and thus out of sight of Mers-el-Kebir to the east.

As they climbed up the hill on their way back, they saw the British battle fleet approaching at a leisurely pace from the west. Amongst those ships Putz spotted the familiar shape of HMS *Hood* which had served with them in the Atlantic and was regarded by them as almost a 'chummy ship'. There she was now flanked by two other battleships of the line and the aircraft carrier *Ark Royal* in company. What was it all about?

There was anxiety also on board the *Hood*. It was now after 0800 and *Foxhound* had already been two hours at Mers-el-Kebir. What was going on? In general, ships at sea in wartime maintain a strict radio silence and Admiral Somerville was not yet in visual touch with his delegate. In the meantime the safety of Force H depended very largely on the reconnaissance of the

Swordfish and Skua aircraft which had been flown off on patrol from *Ark Royal.*

These patrols, which were to continue all day, had begun just before dawn when at 0458 two Swordfish had been flown off to search westward of the fleet during the dawn period. At daylight these aircraft became the fleet's anti-submarine patrol.

Then at 0530, just before *Foxhound*'s arrival off Mers-el-Kebir, six Swordfish had been flown off to screen north-east and north-west to a depth of 150 miles or to the Spanish coast with the object of reporting any Italian or French warships which might be at sea. At the same time three Skuas became airborne forming a fighter escort for Force H with orders to engage any aircraft which might threaten the Fleet.

An hour later a single Swordfish was sent to reconnoitre the harbours of Mers-el-Kebir and Oran and to assist *Foxhound* if required. The value of this may well have been questionable. The Swordfish was a biplane of antique design, perhaps best described as the Fleet Air Arm's maid of all work. Even in 1940 it could be outpaced and outmanœuvred by almost all the aircraft the French had available.

However, no French air activity and indeed no unusual naval movement was observed. But the continual presence of these British aircraft and the fact that the whole area was under surveillance rapidly became an irritant to the French. This waspish annoyance continued as the day wore on.

At 0815 the French Chief of Staff's barge drew smartly alongside HMS *Foxhound* and Lieutenant Dufay was welcomed aboard. After the usual naval courtesies had been briefly exchanged, Commander Peters led his visitor below. Dufay met Holland for the first time that day just as the latter was coming up on deck from the wardroom flat. Holland carried an official briefcase and the two men exchanged a warm greeting, half in English and half in French.

'Thank you for sending a boat so promptly,' Holland said, 'and for coming yourself to take me on board the flagship.'

'I'm sorry,' Dufay said quickly, 'but that won't be possible. The Commander-in-Chief sends his compliments but under the terms of the armistice he cannot allow any British warship the facilities of the port.'

'That's not why I'm here. I have proposals of the utmost importance to make verbally to Admiral Gensoul. It is essential I see him.'

'My orders are to accept any documents you may have for the C.-in-C. If verbal explanation is necessary, Admiral Gensoul is prepared to send his Chief of Staff on board to meet you.'

Holland's initial irritation was now changing into a cold anger. Necessary protocol had already degenerated into needless red tape and he had not yet made a single step towards the real object of his mission. But he kept his temper. 'Although I was merely a Lieutenant and he a four ringed post Captain,' Dufay afterwards reported, 'although at least twenty years in age and experience lay between us, at no time did Captain Holland trade on his rank. He was at all times a self-controlled well-mannered English gentleman for whom I had the greatest respect.'

'This is absurd,' Holland went on after a pause. 'I have these most important documents to deliver personally to Admiral Gensoul. I'm instructed to clarify them verbally. In such circumstances there is no point whatever in my meeting the Chief of Staff. I have clear orders to negotiate with no one except the Commander-in-Chief.'

'I'm sorry but I have my orders too.'

'Very well then. Go back to the Commander-in-Chief and report what I've just told you.'

Dufay saluted and turned away.

'And do your best to get him to see me personally – please.'

This first meeting took ten minutes and by 0825 Dufay was back in the barge *en route* to the flagship. By this time the majority of the French Fleet knew that Captain Holland had been sent to confer with their Commander-in-Chief and that a British Fleet was at large off Oran 'ready to welcome them'.

The blackmail, as it came to be regarded by the French, had begun. It took Dufay twenty minutes to reach the *Dunkerque* which, as flagship, was berthed innermost in the harbour. He found his Admiral and the Chief of Staff extremely angry. Now things began to happen at speed.

To the astonishment of the French Fleet in port, the order *prendre les dispositions de combat* was hoisted by the flagship. This caused initial confusion. Here they were preparing to demobilise and the order for Action Stations was suddenly given. The bewilderment was in part caused by the known fact of North African reservists having already been demobilised and the confusion because at that moment, except for one British destroyer and a circling aircraft, no obvious reason for 'Action Stations' came to the mind.

Certainly it made no sense to Commander Pillet in a destroyer on the inshore side of the harbour. Pillet was at that time the Chief Staff Officer to the Destroyer Flotillas of the French Atlantic Fleet. Work had already begun to remove warheads from torpedoes and breech blocks from the guns of the Division. Half the ship's company of the *Tigre*, the destroyer from which he worked, were ashore bathing.

'Take a boat and go over to the *Provence*,' his Captain told him, 'and find out from Admiral Bouxin what's going on.'

On arrival on board the old battleship, he found Admiral Bouxin pacing the Quarterdeck. Bouxin was an imposing Admiral of the old school who had a habit of clearing his throat as he talked so that the effect was almost syncopated. Pillet saluted and asked why they had all been alerted.

'Is it the Italians?' he asked hopefully. 'Are we going to have a go at the Italians?'

'No,' Bouxin coughed noisily, 'it's . . . hrrmph . . . it's the English.'

On board the *Strasbourg*, commanded by the Breton *Capitaine de Vaisseau* Collinet, the arrival of Captain Holland in Mers-el-

Kebir was greeted with pleasure. Rosset, the First Lieutenant of the *Strasbourg*, suggested that they signal the *Foxhound* and ask him to lunch. This attitude was soon to change.

It was not until he had returned aboard *Dunkerque* after his first meeting with Holland, that Dufay had a sight of the actual wording of the signal which was now common knowledge to the French Fleet. 'Am sending Captain Holland to confer with you . . . the British Fleet is at sea off Oran waiting to welcome you.'

Predictably his Admiral and the Chief of Staff were raw and angry, and after rereading the signal he thought this understandable.

'The English may consider this as bringing friendly pressure to bear,' Gensoul said, 'but the presence of a British Fleet comprising three battleships and an aircraft carrier is something else. This proposal that I should sail my Fleet and join them merits no further examination. And a British Fleet at large off Oran is a menace. I will not be threatened in this way. I've told the British destroyer to get out at once.'

This order was received on board *Foxhound* at 0847. 'To *Foxhound* from *Amiral Atlantique. Vous prie vouloir bien appareiller plus tôt que possible. Signé, Amiral Gensoul.*' Holland's reaction was immediate.

'I'll go in myself in the motorboat,' he said. 'Weigh anchor and give the appearance of complying with the request to sail but take your time. Meanwhile make a signal to the French Admiral to the effect that I'm already on my way in.'

So the *Foxhound*'s motorboat, not in those days a destroyer's most reliable piece of equipment, was duly lowered and at 0905 Holland accompanied by Spearman and Davies set off for the entrance to the boom. It was already scorching hot.

On board the destroyer hands were fallen in for leaving harbour and an ostentatious display of weighing anchor was begun. John Hooker, *Foxhound*'s tall and somewhat piratical-looking First Lieutenant, initiated a piece of perfidious British deceit. As each few shackles were hoisted in on one side of the fo'c'sle, a few more were quietly let go on the other. Thus the *status quo* was maintained. *Foxhound* was apparently complying with the order to sail but getting nowhere in the process.

Meanwhile the news that Captain Holland was *en route* to the flagship reached the French Commander-in-Chief. He reacted with speed. Dufay was immediately despatched in the barge to intercept the British and turn them back. The invaders were not to be allowed into the harbour or on board any French ship. It was like a bad attack of the plague. At about the same time Force H became visible to every ship at Mers-el-Kebir and Oran and began steaming slowly up and down, making occasional legs to seaward.

Whilst the British party in its sturdy but not very dignified motorboat chugged in towards the *Dunkerque*, watched as it seemed by the entire French Atlantic Fleet, and as the much faster French barge sped to intercept them between the inner boom and the breakwater, Gensoul decided that any counter action that was feasible must now be taken. But what was this to be?

He and his Chief of Staff discussed the reasons for the British arrival from every conceivable angle. In defining it he was later to write: 'Essentially the British ultimatum was expressing the fear of seeing our ships pass into the hands of the enemy whereas I knew that this eventuality would never be realised in view of the preparations to scuttle already taken and my own determination to do everything to avoid it. I had already made this quite clear to Admiral Dudley North. At this moment I still considered that the English were only bringing moral pressure to bear on us and that they would never employ force, but I was fully determined, given the form of ultimatum, not to bow to this threat for the honour of the French flag.'

So, as the next meeting between Holland and Dufay was about to take place, the order went out from the French Commander-in-Chief to light all boilers as soon as possible and raise steam for full power. It was apparent, therefore, to the ships and vessels of the French Fleet that their Admiral was playing for time and might later on be intending to make a dash for it.

At this juncture few people, either British or French, believed that anything more than a parley was under way. Dispositions were simply being made by both sides in what could be regarded as a somewhat elaborate nautical game of chess where the rules and the etiquette had not been properly established. There was rising anger at the British presence and at the surveillance by ship and aircraft to which they were being subjected. But this presence was comprehensible. A few days before they had been comrades in arms fighting a common enemy. How could this change overnight? Perhaps, in spite of the armistice, they were going to link up with the British on a joint operation against the Italians. . . .

On board the *Hood* Admiral Somerville assessed the situation now that Force H was on the spot. He had to grope his way through a number of unknown factors and control the impatience which events – or rather non-events – were already engendering.

He had had a shrewd idea that Gensoul would play for time from the start. He thought this natural enough. It was a prime defensive reaction. It all depended, though, on what the French Admiral was going to do with the time he gained from obstructiveness and delay. Ask the advice of other French authorities? Pass the buck to Admiral Darlan? He could guess what the answer would be if that were to happen. Try and make a dash for it? He had no wish to confront the French Fleet at sea. Not only were the two fleets more or less evenly matched, with a possible advantage lying on the French side, but this would also mean that further negotiation had become impossible and that the French Atlantic Fleet might well end up in Toulon or at the bottom of the sea. This was the exact opposite of the result the British authorities were trying to secure, and would only benefit the Germans.

So what was to be done? Shortly after Force H's arrival, one of *Ark Royal*'s aircraft reported that the French battleships were furling awnings and raising steam. This again was the normal reaction to be expected from any warship caught off guard in harbour. But what if they should attempt to sail? Provision had been made for the dropping of magnetic mines from the air in the swept channel off the harbour mouth, but this was a dangerous and delicate operation. Moreover, since the paramount object of the ultimatum was to get the French Fleet to join up with the British, it was perhaps undesirable to blow them up in the process of attempting to do so.

Somerville paced up and down on the Admiral's bridge, exchanging witticisms and pointed remarks with his staff on the minutiae of the day. In personality Somerville was an active, sharp-minded extrovert who relished the reputation he had for being something of a showman. This was in the great tradition stemming from at least as far back as Nelson. A measure of showmanship is a necessary ingredient in the make-up of any great leader.

Somerville had this 'star quality' and in a naval context this was expressed by incessantly working his brain and constantly keeping alert his staff and indeed his entire fleet. He was possessed of a racy humour. He relished a quick response to a joke and if this should be on the blue side, he did not consider it to detract in any way from his dignity.

Like another famous Admiral, John D. Kelly, with whom he had served and who had been largely responsible for restoring morale in the Home Fleet after the Invergordon mutiny, Somerville understood the way naval officers and ratings thought. He knew how to rivet upon himself the sort of intense loyalty which gets results at sea. Force H had not been in existence long enough for his personality to have its full effect but his reputation had preceded him.

The British have a great taste for eccentricity when this is a true expression of individuality and Admiral Somerville was a man of passionate drive and energy, leavened by humanity and humour. In later operations Somerville was always to have with him on the bridge Figaro, his Siamese cat, and Tweet, the canary. He would also occupy the endless periods of waiting by doing crossword puzzles at which his staff were expected to be as adept as himself. Today, however, he had none of these little ameliorations to the harsh realities of a naval operation which privately he detested from the bottom of his heart.

Chapter 6

Back in Whitehall Churchill began the day, as was his wont, by reading the night's telegrams, the Cabinet papers and the news-papers whilst taking his breakfast in bed. The operation of seizing the French ships in British ports had been a success and this he would report to the Cabinet at the daily meeting at 11.15.

Ominously no news had come in, however, from the Commanders-in-Chief at either end of the Mediterranean and accordingly Churchill initiated what was to become during the day a crescendo of increasingly irritated inquiry. He had no fear of applying the goad. He was well aware of the reluctance of those detailed to carry out the operation but in a matter of this magnitude feelings were not allowed to count. Time was not on his side.

Nor, for that matter, was it really on the side of the French. The move from Bordeaux to Vichy had caused Admiral Darlan to become virtually *incommunicado* during that crucial fore-noon of the 3rd July. He had established his main command post, during the move, at Nérac, a town some eighty miles south-east of Bordeaux where, coincidentally, he had been born. It was through Nérac that such radio communication as was permitted to the French Admiralty was effected.

This was not easy and signal traffic was kept to a minimum. Not that there was much to signal about when the day in question opened. The hour-to-hour conduct of affairs had been left in the hands of the Chief of Staff, Rear-Admiral Le Luc, at Nérac with his mobile W/T trucks, but very little was happen-ing now that the armistice was an established fact.

Darlan had set off for Clermont-Ferrand the previous evening and the arrival of Force H off Mers-el-Kebir coincided with one of those moments known to anyone who has been in the armed services, when complete disorganisation in fact exists but which, under normal circumstances and with reasonable luck, would pass without the outside world becoming aware of it and without disaster. Unfortunately the third of July 1940 was a day in which no one got away with anything.

Meanwhile at Mers-el-Kebir the two small boats containing the British emissaries and the French Flag Lieutenants were approaching each other like knights at a medieval joust. Holland was determined to penetrate to the French flagship, Dufay to head him off. They met just inside the boom and both boats then secured to a buoy some 200 yards from the French tug which opened and closed the net defences to the harbour. It was now 0915 and the sun beat down pitilessly on both protagonists.

'I'm afraid the Admiral won't see you,' Dufay said, 'and I have orders to prevent you, if necessary by force, from entering the harbour.'

This was a slight euphemism since they were already inside the harbour, but Holland bowed to the inevitable. For a moment or so he had considered crashing on willy nilly, but a destroyer's unarmed and somewhat underpowered motorboat was not the most effective conveyance in which to take so peremptory a line.

Both Holland and Dufay, who had a high regard for each other, were by this time in a growing state of tension. Both had been given clear orders which were personally odious but imperative. Both, even in this early hour, were dimly aware of what failure to reach an understanding might entail. At this point, though, only Holland, a Captain in the Royal Navy and privy to the power politics thinking of the British Government, really appreciated how the day might end. This in part explained the fact that, although he spoke French better than Dufay English, his expertise in the language deserted him and the ten-minute negotiation which followed was conducted mainly in English. Moreover, no breeze cooled them and the appalling heat lay over them like a suffocating blanket.

They spoke initially from boat to boat, the French Chief of Staff's barge being in relationship to the destroyer motorboat a battleship to a cruiser.

'Perhaps I could come aboard your barge,' Holland said, 'so that we can talk in private.'

It was slightly cooler on board the French vedette. In the discussion which followed neither man was disloyal to the dictates of their respective services. However, they did talk off the record and as friends which, as two very different men of similar training who found themselves facing each other in a situation of potential disaster, they were in duty bound to do.

Had the decision been up to Dufay and Holland, there is little doubt that the day would have ended in a very different manner. The men on the spot do sometimes have more wisdom than their distant masters. But service behaviour is one thing, politics another. Politically they had the freedom of movement of a ping-pong ball riding the jet of water at a fairground shooting booth. Their margin to deviate was virtually nil and both of them knew it.

'Are you certain the Admiral won't see me?' Holland asked. Dufay nodded.

'He's angry – naturally. His pride is offended and his mind is made up.'

Time was dripping away and Holland saw he had reached a dead end. He put his hand into his briefcase and brought out a sealed envelope addressed to *Monsieur l'Amiral Gensoul*. With a sad look in his eyes he passed it over to the French Lieutenant.

'Then give him this. These are the alternatives I hoped to explain to him personally. I'll wait here in *Foxhound*'s motorboat for his answer.'

'I'm afraid there won't be any reply,' Dufay said, and when Holland had left, took the barge across to the tug. There he instructed the Captain of the vessel to keep a gun unobtrusively trained on the British motorboat and to open fire immediately if any further attempt to reach the *Dunkerque* should be made.

By 0930 Dufay was back on board the flagship and had delivered the British document into his Admiral's hands. The flagship was already alive with activity. The ship itself was being prepared for sea almost by stealth and certainly with the minimum observable deck activity since even at this early hour the Commander-in-Chief had decreed that nothing must be done to provoke hasty action by the British.

The Admiral's cabin was also the focal point for senior officers of the Fleet who had come aboard to find out what was going on. But as yet no one, not even the Commander-in-Chief himself, knew for certain what was being asked of them.

From the British point of view the negotiation or rather the non-negotiation had already proceeded by the worst possible route. The means of securing a highly delicate political decision which, Churchill hoped, would be taken by one naval officer after the maximum of personal and professional persuasion by another, now lay on Gensoul's desk like a malignant pill to which no one had bothered to apply a sugar coating. The ultimatum, ironically headed an *aide-mémoire*, was in the wrong language and had to vie for the French C.-in-C.'s attention with the counter action it was urgently necessary for him to think out and order.

On this piece of paper the tragedy hinged. The document was lengthy. A good half of it was taken up by an exposé from the British angle of the political situation, which was worse than useless since neither the French nor the British Admiral could alter political decisions and indeed had no means of judging the accuracy of what was being claimed.

Gensoul therefore reacted, as would any trained naval officer by ignoring the political argument and by despatching a brief and urgent warning signal to the French Admiralty which summarised the situation facing him at 0945. 'English force comprising three battleships, an aircraft carrier, cruisers and destroyers off Oran. Ultimatum sent: Sink your ships in six hours or we shall use force. Reply: French ships will reply to force with force.'

At Nérac this extraordinary piece of news set off a small

volcano of activity. Admiral Darlan, looking for new head-quarters two hundred miles away across the Massif Central in the area of Clermont-Ferrand, could not be contacted. Le Luc, who after all was only a Rear-Admiral, had been left no orders to cover the eventuality now facing him.

He tried to reach his Chief, by every means in his power. Darlan could not be found. Eventually le Luc got through to a Captain Négadelle who passed the news to the Admiral of the Fleet. However, some two hours elapsed before the French Admiralty could react with suitable authority and two hours on a morning such as this felt like half a lifetime to those on the spot.

Back at Mers-el-Kebir Admiral Gensoul, thinking it better to hold the British delegate at arm's length and to play for time, also decided to keep the record straight by sending Holland a reasoned reply.

'The conclusions of this British *aide-mémoire*,' he said to Danbé and Dufay, 'are totally unacceptable. If the British are threatening us with force, our ships must defend themselves with force. You had better take a reply to Captain Holland as follows –'

He paused while Dufay picked up one of the pink signal pads used for secret messages and prepared to take dictation. The reply itself was terse and to the point:

'1° *Les assurances données par l'Amiral Gensoul à l'Amiral Sir Dudley North demeurent entières. En aucun cas, les bâtiments français ne tombereont intacts aux mains des Allemands ni des Italiens.*

2° *Etant donné le fond et la forme du véritable ultimatum qui a été remis à l'Amiral Gensoul, les bâtiments français se défendront par la force.*'

So at 1000 Dufay was again in the dark blue barge *en route* to the harbour mouth on his third trip that morning with instructions to furnish Captain Holland, in the most forcible and unequivocal terms, with any additional explanation he might seek.

Meanwhile *Ark Royal*'s aircraft, having reported that all

battleships, cruisers and destroyers in Mers-el-Kebir had furled awnings and were raising steam, a little later gave Admiral Somerville the estimate that the French Fleet would be ready for sea by 12.30. Four hours had already elapsed since the day had begun, and one hour since Force H had made its visible presence felt. The signals from London were already expressing impatience and Somerville had no progress whatever to report. The pressure of frustration was steadily increasing and to a man of Somerville's temperament the failure to get things moving, indeed to get a reaction of any sort was galling.

On board the *Dunkerque*'s sister ship, the 26,000-ton *Strasbourg*, Captain Collinet called his officers together and told them that they must be prepared to sail and to fight. 'I know the British,' he said. 'They mean what they say. If they cannot persuade us to join them, they will certainly attempt to sink us. Therefore as soon as we are ordered or as soon as the first shot is fired, we sail for Toulon.'

The *Strasbourg* was what the Royal Navy called a 'private ship', that is, she carried no Admiral or staff on board. The *Dunkerque*, on the other hand, was not only berthed inmost to the shore, she was also cluttered up with over a hundred extra officers and men of the *majorité* as the *Etat-Major* was known.

She was thus at a double disadvantage. She had farther to go getting out of Mers-el-Kebir, and should it be necessary to shoot from the harbour, the high bulk of Fort Santon severely limited her arc of fire. *Dunkerque* was also hampered in this tense situation by the additional staff personnel she carried who, from the point of view of fighting the ship, were passengers.

Theoretically an Admiral and his staff take no part in the organisation and running of a flagship but theory is one thing, human nature another. Interference, sometimes obvious, sometimes subtle, is almost inevitable, especially since the flagship must always lead, must always be the smartest ship of the fleet.

As the day progressed the *Dunkerque* suffered from a sort of to-and-fro, stop and start atmosphere caused on the one hand

93

by the need to get the ship ready to sail in fighting trim and on the other by not appearing to be doing anything of the kind. The C.-in-C. had laid down that there must be no overt provocation of the British. However, it is extremely difficult to prepare a large battleship for sea without parties of men working on deck. Anchor cables have to be shortened in and the mooring hawsers which hold the ship to the mole made ready for instant slipping. The Flag Captain and Commandant Tanguy were not having an easy day.

When Dufay had previously returned to the flagship with the blunt British ultimatum in his hand, his last words had been, 'I'm afraid there won't be any reply.' This could well have been so. How long, therefore, was Holland to give it before deciding on other action? And what action was possible other than going back to *Foxhound* and giving up?

He watched the French Admiral's barge speed back to the *Dunkerque* at 0920 and he reckoned that his *aide-mémoire* must have been read by Gensoul in less than a quarter of an hour. Surely, he thought, the gravity of the British demand and the previous Franco-British relationship would merit a summons to himself to repair on board the French flagship? A short signal would have sufficed. They kept their eyes glued to the signal deck of the French flagship. But nothing happened.

For the next half-hour, from 0930 until close on 1000, Holland and his party were in limbo. Their little motorboat rocked gently at its buoy, the seagulls wheeled and cawed overhead and all around them the great French Fleet was, to their expert eyes, quite clearly preparing for action.

If Gensoul had decided to ignore the British ultimatum, which to Holland was understandable and which was what Dufay thought would happen, then a confrontation of the two fleets at sea would be inevitable. The idea sickened him and it must have gone through Holland's mind a number of times during that growing period of uncertainty that perhaps he should have obeyed his original instinct to refuse the whole task, which had caused him an agonising forenoon at Gibraltar.

So his spirits rose when he saw the Commander-in-Chief's barge speeding back towards them. They had not been forgotten. The mid-morning heat was more oppressive than ever and there was no relief for any of them. But at least the boat approaching them conveyed some sort of emblem of hope.

'I came alongside *Foxhound*'s motorboat at about 1000,' Dufay wrote in his report. 'They were still secured to the same buoy and had made no attempt to penetrate further into the harbour. Captain Holland at once asked if he could cross over and discuss matters with me in the cabin of the barge so as to avoid being overheard by the other officers with him or by the boat's crew.

'I agreed to this with some astonishment. I had expected our conference to be conducted in French, a language Captain Holland knows well, whereas my notions of English are summary. As it turned out, the English language was almost the only one used throughout this interview in the course of which Captain Holland appeared to be extremely ill at ease, in a state of anxiety, pale and searching for words. The torrid temperature in the cabin of the barge was certainly not enough to explain this physical, intellectual and moral condition. . . .'

In his own report Captain Holland made no comment on this emotional pressure and it would have been out of character if he had. But he was undoubtedly in a high state of nerves. Moreover, as soon as Dufay had handed over his Admiral's reply, the sombre feeling of disaster returned . . . 'owing to the form of this "veritable ultimatum" the French ships would defend themselves by force' – which a glance round the harbour only too obviously confirmed.

'I then asked the Flag Lieutenant to sit down and discuss the matter as old friends,' Holland wrote in his narrative of events. 'I said he must take back to the Admiral a copy of what I had proposed saying at my interview.'

At least both men could trust each other. It was only a straw to clutch at but there was space for a change of mind. The nominal expiry time for the ultimatum lay four hours ahead. There were still possibilities of solution.

'Admiral Gensoul told me to emphasise to you the essential part of this message,' Dufay said, '*En aucun cas les bâtiments français ne tomberont intacts aux mains des Allemands ni des Italiens* – in no case will French ships fall intact into the hands of the Germans or Italians He said would you please take note that the term "*en aucun cas*" means any time, anywhere, anyway and without further orders from the French Admiralty. These are Admiral Darlan's orders.'

'Yes. We know about that. But those instructions were drafted before the armistice was signed. Suppose you now receive an order cancelling them?'

'It would not be obeyed.'

'No?'

'No!'

The two men looked at each other, both of them aware of the highly secret code arranged by Darlan before the armistice but neither of them able to bring this out into the open. There was a pause.

'We had better be quite frank with each other,' Holland said, 'I'm trusting you as a comrade and a friend. We know of the existence of your Admiralty's signals 5057, 5058 and 5059 of the 20th June, which read as follows . . .' he consulted some papers in his briefcase:

To all Senior Officers of the French Fleet.

1. The Admiral of the Fleet believes that he may be able to retain command of naval forces and is taking steps to ensure as much.

2. In the event of the Admiral of the Fleet's being unable to exercise his command freely, naval forces would become subject to the orders of Admiral de Laborde, then of Admiral Estéva, then of Admiral Abrial and next of Admiral Gensoul.

3. All these general officers or those who might be called upon to succeed them will have to comply with the following general orders:

(*a*) Fight fiercely to the last until a true French Government, independent of the enemy, gives orders to the contrary;

(*b*) Disobey any other government;

(*c*) Whatever orders are received, never surrender a warship to the enemy intact.

Dufay, who as Admiral Gensoul's A.D.C. had deciphered these instructions himself, showed no surprise that Holland had a copy of them but waited patiently for the British delegate to reveal that he was aware of another essential piece of information, namely the secret signature 'Xavier 377' authorised by Darlan four days later on 24th June without which any orders emanating from the French Admiralty were suspect and were to be ignored. But Holland made no mention of this and Dufay had no means of knowing whether he was aware of this key factor or not.

'Those orders remain in force,' Dufay said.

'They were issued before the armistice,' Holland said, 'and the British Government believes that the situation of Admiral Darlan being no longer able to exercise effective command has now come about.'

Dufay shook his head.

'Then when did you last have a signal – a personally authorised signal from Admiral Darlan?'

'About two days ago. The French Admiralty is moving its headquarters from Nérac to Vichy.'

'Did it have the special code word on it?'

Dufay looked at the British captain with surprise. Now it was out.

'Xavier 377.' Holland said.

'You know about that?'

'Yes, we know about that. I must also remind you and through you, Admiral Gensoul, that over the past year I have had a very close association indeed not only with Admiral Darlan himself but with all the French naval staff. I repeat – the British Government believes that the French Admiral of the Fleet, whom I admire and respect, is no longer fully in command and is acting partially or completely under duress. There are many reasons for this. I do not know if you are aware of the signal sent a couple of days ago by the French Admiralty to Algiers ordering preparations to be made for the accommodation of the French Admiralty in that city. Our General Dillon got wind of this. He and Admiral Dudley North deduced from this that Admiral Darlan's hands were tied. In fact he is no longer at liberty to take free and unbiased decisions nor is he able to give orders to his sub-commands with sufficient guarantees of authenticity. From the British point of view this is a completely unacceptable situation.'

'I can't comment on that. I know nothing of this signal and I don't see what it has to do with the present ultimatum.'

'This is one of the things I intended to discuss with Admiral Gensoul. Since we are talking as friends, I must tell you that in my opinion the *aide-mémoire* I was compelled to give you an hour ago is clumsy and maladroit in essence and in form. This, in fact, is the point of my mission – to explain to your Commander-in-Chief that he must not look on it as an ultimatum but rather as an expression of hope. What I intended to do was to persuade Admiral Gensoul that we are trying to do everything we possibly can to help him out of a very difficult situation. But how can I do this if I can't even get to see him face to face?'

'But it is the threat of force . . .,' Dufay said, somewhat embarrassed by the fact that the British Captain was obviously in great distress, hesitant, pale and sweating profusely. Dufay could see no reason other than a sort of desperation for the last ten minutes to have been taken up by arguments '*aussi dépourvus de valeur*' and without any direct bearing on the matter in hand. Both men were highly keyed up.

'I did not speak,' Dufay wrote in his report, 'until my interlocutor, at the end of his breath – and perhaps his ideas – fell silent. Certain of expressing the opinion of my chiefs, I then declared to him that, as he could surely be in no doubt, we *had* taken precautions to prevent our ships falling intact into enemy hands. I added that a rupture of communications with the Admiral of the Fleet, whilst admitting that this had indeed just come about, would put no obstacle in the way of executing such orders.'

'These measures,' he again emphasised to the British Captain, 'have been decentralised down to ship level and you can be absolutely sure, without any possibility of misunderstanding, that in the event they will be put into force "any time, anywhere, anyway and without further orders from the French Admiralty" as I told you before.'

The French Commander-in-Chief wrote his report of proceedings on 'The aggression at Mers-el-Kebir' on 9th July – six days after the events took place. The document was factual, the comment limited and sober, the high drama which unrolled during the day reduced to a cool, accurate narrative of events. A month afterwards – on 2nd August 1940 – the Flag Lieutenant wrote for his Admiral a *'Compte-Rendu des missions exécutées par le Lieutenant de Vaisseau Dufay'* which, even after this period of reflection, and precisely and calmly written though it was, conveyed vividly the pressure of emotion in which this tragedy took place.

'I remain convinced,' he recorded 'and I shall return to this later, that Captain Holland was trying loyally to find a solution to an insoluble problem.'

Having exhausted the general political argument which, as Dufay pointed out, was not what they were there to discuss, a brief pause ensued, after which Holland set off on a new tack.

'We are not putting into question your good faith in any shape or form,' he went on. 'Nor do we doubt your resolve to execute your commitments loyally. However, the British Government does have a considerable doubt about your ability to withstand a German or Italian attack on your ships.'

Dufay made no comment but waited for him to go on.

'What worries us most of all is the disarmament of your ships in a French metropolitan port. Suppose that instead of Oran, the Fleet is disarmed at Toulon. What sort of destruction, sabotage or sinking could possibly be done by crews of ships effectively reduced to a "care and maintenance" basis? You would be surrounded by enemy forces – greatly superior forces – of every kind. These would not only hamper your ability to act but might also try to seize control of your ships with every chance of success.'

'That possibility has been foreseen and taken care of in the orders given to the ships.'

'It may have been foreseen but what guarantee of effectiveness can there possibly be?'

Except that they were talking off the record and as friends, this was an unfair question for a British four-ringed Captain to ask of a junior French Lieutenant. Indeed it was impossible to answer. What guarantee could there be in the conditions of an unknown, complex situation which might or might not come about?

'Our home port for disarmament purposes has not yet been fixed,' Dufay said. 'but *a priori* no serious objection has been made to the choice of Mers-el-Kebir.'

'Simply because for the moment the Germans may have enough on their hands, it may suit them to let this matter ride. But both our nations have had enough experience of Hitler's treachery not to trust overmuch in the German word of honour. The moment it becomes expedient, they will seize your ships – and what could you do about it? This is what is causing us such deep anxiety and that is why we are here today. There is all the difference in the world between disarming at Toulon and doing it here in Oran.'

It was this insistence which created a sudden glint of hope and which enabled Dufay to suspect that this might be an area of possible negotiation.

'But I did not consider myself qualified,' he wrote, 'to go more deeply into this in the name of the Admiral. I was on a path where the slightest false step might cause a catastrophe so I said as little as possible and asked to be released, since the essential part of my mission had been completed.'

In fact, he could not wait to get away. This was a natural reaction but it was not going to be as easy as that. Holland saw the presence of the Flag Lieutenant as his single link, albeit the size of a thread, with common sense, understanding and sanity in a situation which could slip away into total disaster almost at the blink of an eye. He had to think rapidly. Conventional procedure, rank, protocol, the careful preparations he had made the night before for the negotiations he thought he was going to conduct with the French Commander-in-Chief –

all these had long ago gone overboard. Now Dufay was about to return to the flagship and they were no whit nearer a solution of the dilemma facing both sides.

'Very well,' Holland said, after a pause in which he had rapidly reassessed the situation. 'Since your Admiral obstinately refuses even to see me, I must ask you to take back with you now the notes I was going to use at the interview. Read them yourself on your way back to the flagship – since no doubt you will need to translate them into French for the Commander-in-Chief.'

He handed over a couple of sheets of typed paper and gave the Flag Lieutenant a cool look:

'And please do your very best for the sake of all of us to impress on the Commander-in-Chief our point of view, the reasons for our acute anxiety and the goodwill we are anxious to show. This may well be our only hope and time is running out.'

Holland then returned to the *Foxhound's* motorboat along-side and a few moments later the French vedette set off back to the *Dunkerque*. As before, the French barge speeding back to the flagship and the British motorboat still secured to its buoy became the cynosure of the French Fleet.

Overhead, aircraft from HMS *Ark Royal* droned away, circling and wheeling on their endless watch. In the harbour itself the occasional bugle sounded from the warships at anchor as the day's routine continued. Sudden wisps of smoke and steam from the funnels confirmed that, out of sight in the boiler rooms, power for full speed was being raised. Inter-mittent clonks sounded from across the calm oily water of the harbour as capstans were tested and anchor chains shifted.

Ships' boats with officers standing importantly in the stern sheets fussed to and fro from ship to ship and the tugs and lighters, essential to the preparation of a fleet for sea, moved about their business. By now everyone in the French Fleet knew that something really important was afoot but only senior officers had knowledge of the vital issue at stake. Unlike the British ships out in the bay, the French lower deck was not kept informed by internal broadcasting of what it was all about. They were left much more to guesswork and rumour, but resentment against the British presence and particularly against the surveillance of the Swordfish and Skua aircraft steadily increased. It was 1025.

Chapter 7

Communication, or rather the lack of it, became crucial in that convulsive summer of 1940 and this was epitomised at Mers-el-Kebir. At the top political level the fall of France ruptured any real accord between the two greatest nations then fighting the German and Italian dictatorships. The consequent collapse of this relationship rapidly brought on distrust and recrimination on either side. Both England and France had valid reasons for thinking and feeling as they did.

Until Dunkirk the seagoing working arrangements between the French and British navies had been excellent. Indeed, from September 1939 until May 1940 action at sea had provided almost the only brightness in an otherwise gloomy and static 'phoney war'. The first rift appeared at Dunkirk. The operation was nominally under the control of Admiral Abrial, an elderly officer with the full Maginot line mentality.

According to the British, Abrial took shelter in the fortress at Dunkirk, became inaccessible and thus largely unaware of the progress of events. The British, upon whom the successful evacuation essentially depended, were certainly no troglodytes and it was this basic divergence in outlook which grew and came to a climax at Mers-el-Kebir. General Spears, who was Churchill's man in France at that time, put it bluntly enough. 'The Admiral was no doubt a naturally brave man, but a thirty-foot shell of concrete endowed him with the confidence and aggressiveness of a rhinoceros and his vision was as limited. He at any rate could not be sunk whatever happened to the transports outside.' It is small wonder that Spears, who loved the French, did not always find his affection returned.

Darlan protested to the British Admiralty about the way 'in

which it seems to have lost interest in the outcome of the Battle of Dunkirk now that the British contingents are safe' – a remark which was neither true nor calculated to improve relationships at that terrible time. Indeed, as Spears and Campbell, the British Ambassador to France, had individually and frequently reported, there were strong and increasing anti-British influences in the French Cabinet and High Command. Of these the most dangerous was undoubtedly Laval, whose loathing of the British was almost pathological, but the mistresses of Reynaud, the Prime Minister, and of Daladier, the Minister of Defence, were also cool towards the Anglo-Saxons.

Admiral Auphan, the distinguished historian, who was present at the heart of these events, says: 'There was a time when the Fleet would have been able, without hesitation and under discipline, to pass to the Allies. That was the 16th June. There were politicians then who thought that the Fleet should have sailed for England at that time. There was then no political objection nor blood spilt between us and our allies. The Fleet in its entirety could have been sent without trouble to allied ports if the regular Minister of Marine in the Cabinet, of which General de Gaulle was a member, had given the order.'

But no such order was forthcoming and the opportunity passed. In this the role of Darlan was decisive. He was then Chief of the Naval Staff and Campinchi still Minister of Marine. But Darlan told him nothing.

As Spears reported: 'Campinchi did not know much more about the French Fleet than I did. This was in the French tradition but it was a pity that – loyal, plucky and intelligent though he was – of the two men at the head of the Navy, it was the politician with neither knowledge nor power who was our true and reliable friend and not the sailor.'

Darlan's real feeling towards England and his reasons for not sending the Fleet to the United Kingdom or America are now unlikely to be known with any certainty, though they can be guessed at and assessed. He was murdered in Algiers at Christmas 1942 shortly after the Anglo-American invasion of North Africa.

There is no doubt that he was a great man who attracted to himself the loyalty and admiration of the vast majority of French naval officers and men. To the British he was and still is an enigma. His great-grandfather, a Petty Officer, had been killed at Trafalgar. There had been an unfortunate discourtesy at King George the Sixth's coronation when, because he was not ranked as an Admiral of the Fleet, he had been seated behind a pillar in Westminster Abbey with a Chinese Admiral. There was justified and continuing resentment at the inferior status accorded the French Navy in the horse-trading over naval power in which England and America indulged in the thirties. Above all to someone born at that epoch, the Entente Cordiale only lightly disguised the centuries-old rivalry between France and England and the general feeling, which always emerged at times of crisis, that England was 'the hereditary enemy'.

By the time Dufay had returned on board the *Dunkerque*, he had digested the notes which Holland had asked him to show the Admiral. He did not think they were going to alter the scene in any material way. However, he told his Admiral briefly what had taken place at his last meeting with Holland and handed over the document as he had been requested to do. He explained that, had Holland been allowed access to the Commander-in-Chief, these notes covered what he would then have said. Admiral Gensoul sat down at his desk and read them through.

'The British Government have had suspicions for some days,' the typescript began, 'that the Germans and Italians were intending to break the armistice terms as regards the Navy as soon as favourable opportunity occurred. The day before yesterday this was confirmed beyond all doubt. Admiral Somerville, who is commanding the British naval forces at Gibraltar and who had many weeks of close co-operation with your ships during the Spanish civil war, has therefore been ordered to present certain proposals to you and has sent me for the purpose.'

105

Admiral Gensoul looked up at his A.D.C.

'What is behind all this?'

'The British think Admiral Darlan is no longer able to speak except under duress.'

The Admiral considered this for a moment and then went on with his reading.

'This intended action is a dastardly trick which reacts as much against us as it does against you. I have told you here more than I have been ordered to do, but having had the honour of serving with the French Navy and directly under the orders of its Chief, who trusted me and gave me his friendship, I feel I wish to help in every way I can. Because of my close associations with you, I perhaps realise and feel more acutely the circumstances from your point of view. But I must also try and put our point of view to you, if I am permitted to do so.'

'What is the point of all this?' Gensoul said, almost as if asking a rhetorical question. 'How can I be expected to take political decisions?'

Neither the Flag Lieutenant nor the Chief of Staff had any suggestion to make so Gensoul returned to his study of the document.

'It goes without saying that we trust your Chief and your Admirals in high commands who have spoken for the French Navy. Thus, on the 18th June, Admiral Darlan gave a personal promise to the First Lord and First Sea Lord that the French Fleet would never surrender to the enemy. A few days later I understand the Admiral of the Fleet sent a telegram to the effect that he hoped personally to maintain command of the French Navy but, should he find himself unable to do so satisfactorily for some unseen reason, he nominated the command successively to Admiral de Laborde, Estéva and yourself.'

'The British are well informed,' the Admiral murmured dryly, and for a moment or so looked into the distance.

'Admiral Estéva's reply to the First Sea Lord about that date was in the same sense and he added that if orders to give up the Fleet were given by the Government, as opposed to the Chief, he would not obey them.'

Gensoul knew this was true. The relationship between the senior Admiral Estéva and Admiral Gensoul was close. In a sense, as Dufay was well aware, Gensoul was the *enfant chéri* – the blue-eyed boy – of the man who held down the job of *Amiral Sud* – the Commander-in-Chief of all the southern Mediterranean and North African naval forces, the Admiral with overall command of Algiers, Bizerta and Oran together with the ships necessary to defend that considerable sector of French power. The Fleet under Admiral Gensoul's command was the *Flotte de Raid*, basically designed, as was Force H, to act as a striking force.

'You, Admiral,' Gensoul read on, 'assured Admiral North in the same sense the other day and Admirals Ollive and de Laborde said the same to me. Thus there is the assurance, one might say, of the French Navy and, Admiral, naturally and very sincerely, we believe you.'

It was ironic to realise that such a statement of trust would have been unnecessary, would indeed have been considered insulting, before the collapse of France. Then the good faith of the French Navy would never have been in question. How were the mighty fallen! It was small wonder that in that historic railway carriage at Compiègne, when the armistice was signed, both General Keitel on the German side and General Huntziger on the French had tears in their eyes. Admiral Gensoul returned to the British delegate's notes.

'But in view of what has been found out with regard to the treachery of the Germans and Italians, with the French Army disarmed and the Fleet laid up with reduced crews under German and Italian surveillance, the Government feels that there can be no certainty that, however resolute the attempt to destroy or sink the ships, it would not be possible to forestall seizure by the enemy.'

This was impugning the French Navy's professional ability even to sink itself and made no sense to Gensoul; apart from its more general implication, which could be taken as a studied insult. In the event both points of view were to be proved correct. Two years later with considerable valour the French ships at Toulon scuttled themselves at the eleventh hour with the Germans almost on board: at Bizerta, on the other hand, the French commander surrendered the port to the Germans intact on a life-or-death ultimatum which he had twenty minutes to accept or refuse.

'Before putting to you the proposals,' Holland's notes went on, 'I will, if I may, give you Admiral Somerville's messages. He sends you his sincere wishes, adding that he has a most happy recollection of his collaboration with the French Navy and that he will always take with him the souvenirs of the many friendships he made.' Then followed the proposals:

(a) To sail with the British Fleet and continue the fight against the Germans and Italians.

(b) To sail with reduced crews under British control to a British port.

(c) To sail with reduced crews to some French port in the West Indies.

[Here I proposed to stop, Holland's notes went on, hoping a discussion on the above would ensue. If nothing came of this then . . .]

If you do not see your way to accepting one of these fair offers, I must with profound regret require you to sink your ships within six hours.

[Again a stop before putting the final terms.]

Finally, failing the above, I have orders from H.M. Government to use whatever force may be necessary to prevent your ships falling into German or Italian hands.

As soon as the Admiral had finished reading the English text, Dufay, who was feeling the effects of his encounters with Captain Holland, asked the Commander-in-Chief not to send him back to the *Foxhound*'s motorboat. He had had enough. Dufay's reason for this was that either the discussion was at an end, in which event it was pointless for the *Aide-Mémoire* to be returned by an officer, or the Admiral would wish to keep open the possibility of further negotiations, in which case it seemed to him more politic for such negotiations to be conducted by an officer of a rank equal to that of the British delegate.

By this time a certain confusion was building up in the Admiral's cabin. The Chief of Staff, Captain Danbé, and his assistant Commander Clatin, were constantly coming and going as points of detail concerning the preparation of the Fleet for sea required the Admiral's decision. Rear-Admirals Lacroix and Bouxin in charge of subdivisions of the Fleet were in attendance and through it all Gensoul had to keep a clear head and decide in his own mind on the best course of action. Already, although no one spotted it at the time, one important detail had been omitted in the first warning signal Gensoul had sent to the French Admiralty.

'What is my explanation,' Gensoul afterwards said, 'for not reproducing more completely in that telegram the terms of the ultimatum, as I later did in my report? I think it was because of the obsession which haunted me at that time that I was really being offered only two alternatives – either to sink my ships or to see them sunk by the English. My only thought was that, as it was absolutely impossible for me to bend to an ultimatum under the threat of English guns, I did not envisage the possibility for a single instant of accepting the offer of seeing my ships sail for the West Indies or the United States under the conduct or the menace of English ships.

'I might, perhaps, have agreed to sail my Fleet to the United States freely, but not with English guns pointed at our ships. At that time I did not reconcile this situation with the third paragraph of the Admiralty's signal of the 24th June. . . . "If the Armistice Commission responsible for interpreting the text were to decide otherwise than that demobilised warships are to remain French, under the French flag with French reduced crews in French metropolitan or colonial ports then . . . in the absence of further orders, warships would be either sailed to the United States or scuttled."

'Perhaps I ought to have thought of it. Perhaps I ought to have transmitted to the Admiralty a more complete extract of the English ultimatum. I still cannot explain why I did not do it nor how it was that the officers in my entourage (Danbé, Clatin – now dead – and Dufay) did not draw my attention to this omission. These telegrams were very hastily drafted and one has to go back to the atmosphere of the time. I do not know if Rear-Admirals Lacroix and Bouxin were actually present when the above telegram was drafted but I had summoned them on board the *Dunkerque* to bring them up to date with the situation.'

After Dufay had pointed out the glint of hope which might possibly exist in disarming the Fleet there on the spot, the certainty grew in Gensoul's mind that he must draw Admiral Somerville's attention to the terrible consequences which the first shots fired against them would bring. Even at this early hour one stark fact stood out like the Rock of Gibraltar and it was this: any use of force in the circumstances then obtaining at Mers-el-Kebir might well result in a declaration of war between France and England. What pleasure this would bring to Hitler and Mussolini! And what incalculable tragedy would follow in its train!

Gensoul turned to his Chief of Staff, 'You had better go and talk to Captain Holland,' he said, 'and take Dufay with you.'

He nodded to his Flag Lieutenant who picked up a signal pad and then took down the following message fired at him in rapid French by the Commander-in-Chief (the original of which is now in the Public Record Office in London). The English translation reported by Captain Holland reads:

1. Admiral Gensoul can but confirm the reply already sent by Lieutenant Dufay;

2. Admiral Gensoul is determined to defend himself by every means possible;

3. Admiral Gensoul wishes to draw Admiral Somerville's attention to the fact that the first shot fired against us will have result of immediately putting the whole French Fleet against Great Britain, a result which is diametrically opposite to that which H.M. Government is seeking.

So, with a heavy heart and this time accompanied by the Chief of Staff, Dufay set off once more in the Admiral's barge.

It was nearly 11 a.m. A slight breeze, force 1-2, as reported by *Ark Royal*'s aircraft drifted in from the north-east, heated by the Mediterranean. A variable visibility of 5-10 miles obtained and over all the summer haze shimmered like an aureole of threat. The malignancy bearing down on them could almost be felt in the air.

Chapter 8

Throughout this first act of the drama Force H was steaming to and fro across the bay, making occasional legs to seaward, with HMS *Ark Royal* acting independently as necessary for the flying on and off of her aircraft. Outwardly it was a tranquil, leisurely scene. To the sailors closed up at cruising stations nothing was happening and, as yet, no one seriously thought the guns would be fired. In accordance with normal practice, Commanding Officers had taken their ships' companies into their confidence and had told them briefly over the tannoy what it was all about.

At the other end of the Mediterranean Admiral Cunningham was achieving a greater measure of success with the French Admiral Godfroy and this fact was passed on by the Admiralty to Force H in the vain hope that it would in some way influence Gensoul. In reality the two situations were completely different.

At Alexandria, a very considerable port under British control, the French ships had been berthed in the inner harbour where, since June, the two fleets had been united under the name of Force X. This berthing in the inner harbour was a shrewd and wise move from the British point of view. Moreover, until the armistice, Admiral Godfroy, whilst naturally obeying the general edicts of the French Admiralty, had been placed under Admiral Cunningham's direct operational command.

It was also fortunate that the two Admirals were on excellent personal terms. When, therefore, on 24th June – the day of the armistice – Darlan ordered the French ships at Alexandria to sail for Beirut, Cunningham refused to allow this to happen but followed his refusal with a letter saying: 'I ask you to accept this situation as inevitable under present circumstances and in truth this may well turn out to be an advantage in the sense that after a few days' delay we shall see things more clearly. . . .

I am confident, my dear Admiral, that my action will not cause any bad feeling between us. I have the greatest sympathy for you in all your difficulties.' The tone was firm but it left a door open for discussions, and between that date and 3rd July a number of both official and private talks took place between the two Admirals.

Thus, on the morning of 3rd July, whilst Admiral Gensoul was stolidly refusing even to receive the British delegate at Mers-el-Kebir, Admiral Godfrey was on board HMS *Warspite* learning from the British Commander-in-Chief in person the conditions of Operation Capatult as they were to be applied to the French ships at Alexandria. He did not like what he was told any more than Gensoul did. Upon reflection, however, he did not feel he was being given an ultimatum. In essence this was, of course, so but the requirements were couched in courteous terms without overt menace and without a time limit being imposed. Cunningham simply told him the British Government were anxious to have his reply 'in a very short time'.

Godfroy then went back on board his flagship and drafted a signal to the French Admiralty reproducing in full, unlike Gensoul, the integral part of the English text. Neither side sounded off 'Action Stations' and Godfroy waited for a reply to his signal which in the event never got through to France.

This situation at Alexandria was to change later in the day when Godfroy learned what had taken place at Mers-el-Kebir. Then a period ensued when the two fleets came within an inch of disaster. At this hour of the morning, however, the British ultimatum at Alexandria appeared to have been successfully put across. Thus Somerville at the other end of the Mediterranean was able to signal to Gensoul that: 'Admiral Godfroy was demilitarising his ships at Alexandria with reduced crews'.

At Mers-el-Kebir a more sombre situation had come about. Whilst the French Chief of Staff and Dufay were *en route* to meet Holland, who was still bobbing about in *Foxhound*'s motor-boat, Admiral Somerville backed up the news from Alexandria by taking another step towards calamity. He signalled *Fox-*

hound: 'Imperative French should know I will not repetition nor allow them to leave harbour unless terms accepted.' By the time this message had been flashed to *Foxhound* a good number of the French ships certainly knew what it was all about.

At this time *Foxhound* was still on the other or sea side of the breakwater, no longer in visual touch with Holland. 'It is important to realise,' the Commanding Officer of *Foxhound* remarked later on, 'that once Captain Holland had gone into the harbour we had no idea of what was going on. This was long before the days of walkie-talkie and because of the height of the mole we could not see the sides of the French ships, only their upperworks.'

The signals passing between Admiral Somerville and *Foxhound* were made in the first instance by light in rapid Morse code. Every French ship or at all events every major ship with a signalman on watch could take down this traffic and therefore, although the information gleaned would not normally be distributed much beyond the Captain and senior officers of the ships concerned, the news in the making was able to spill round most of the French ships in port. The buzz was about, as the British lower deck would then have phrased it.

Thus whilst the meeting between the British delegate and the French Chief of Staff was taking place in the Admiral's barge in the middle of the harbour, the message which had reached *Foxhound* in English was now being transmitted to Admiral Gensoul in French: '*Je regrette de vous informer que conformément à mes ordres je ne vous permettrai pas de sortir du port à moins que les termes du Gouvernement de Sa Majesté ne soient acceptés. Suis informé qu'Amiral Godfroy démilitarise ses bâtiments maintenant à Alexandrie avec équipage réduit.*'

This was the putting together of two signals in English made by Admiral Somerville in HMS *Hood* to Captain Holland in HMS *Foxhound*. Although later these messages were taken in by hand by Lieutenant Commander Spearman and given to Lieutenant Dufay who then took them to Admiral Gensoul, the contents of the communication had already been disseminated to the rest of the French Fleet piecemeal through the process of watching what the British and French Admirals were saying to each other by Aldis lamp.

Meanwhile an hour before high noon the encounter between Holland, Danbé and Dufay was taking place. The conversation was brief, '*et sans observations du Commandant Holland méritant d'être notées*', as Gensoul was to write. Dufay, however, reports that when Danbé had handed over Gensoul's message, ending as it did with its barbed warning that, 'the first shot fired against us would have the practical result of putting the entire French Fleet against Great Britain', Holland remarked to the French Chief of Staff:

'Permit me to say as one officer to another that in your place my reply would not have been different.'

To which Danbé said:

'I think that would also be the opinion of every British Officer.'

'Well,' Holland said after a pause, 'thank you for bringing me this document in person but there seems to be no point in going over the same ground again since your Admiral is determined not to see me. I must get this reply to Admiral Somerville as soon as possible so I shall return on board HMS *Foxhound* straight away. If I have anything further to communicate I shall signal *Dunkerque* and send in the motorboat.'

The two Captains shook hands and took their leave of each other, the French barge speeding back to the *Dunkerque* and the little British motorboat churning its way out of the harbour to the waiting destroyer. The *pourparler* was at an end.

It had been Holland's intention to confer with Admiral Somerville personally, taking *Foxhound* out into the bay and alongside the battlecruiser. However, when he got back on board the destroyer and read the signals which had stacked up since his departure, he decided that there must be no possibility whatever of misunderstanding between himself and Gensoul. The French Admiral would have to be told in writing, plainly and in French, that his ships would not be allowed to sail unless and until one of the British alternatives had been accepted.

So Lieutenant Commander Spearman, 'a dark nervous little

chap' as the Captain of *Foxhound* described him, set off for the *Dunkerque* in the motorboat to deliver the signal set out above. When he reached the *Dunkerque* and went up on the quarter-deck, he was received by the Officer of the Watch, an ironically-minded *Lieutenant de Vaisseau* called André Libiot, who afterwards had one of his lungs burnt out by inhaling high pressure steam. In the normal way of a visitor on board a warship, Spearman saluted and his salute was returned. '*Bonjour, mon nouvel ennemi,*' Libiot said with a smile, as he took delivery of the letter Spearman was bringing. It was still unthinkable that the guns should actually be fired. Spearman then returned to HMS *Foxhound*, the journey there and back taking the better part of an hour.

After the Chief of Staff and the Flag Lieutenant were once more on board the *Dunkerque*, Gensoul decided to take advantage of the inevitable hiatus caused by Holland's declared necessity of conferring with Admiral Somerville. There was time to relax his crews and get them fed.

At 1138, therefore, he cancelled the *branle-bas de combat* (Action Stations) considering that in any case the ultimatum would not be enforced without further warning. This let-up enabled people to eat their midday meal and generally to blow off steam. Curiosity and rumour of every kind were dancing about every mess in every ship of the Fleet. What was it all about? What was going to happen?

The French Admiral's thinking at this time was dominated by two *idées maîtresses*. The first and paramount was to do nothing in any shape or form which could be considered aggressive. Defend themselves, as they certainly would, Gensoul was determined that the French under his command would never fire the first shot since this would risk the outbreak of war between France and Great Britain. The second was tactical – at all costs to gain time and if possible reach nightfall without a decision being forced on either side.

'In effect,' as he wrote in his report, 'every minute gained on the limit of the ultimatum (originally fixed at 1400 hours) allowed:

(*a*) All ships to make the best preparations possible to sail with speed and to prepare for action;

(*b*) Coastal and anti-aircraft batteries to rearm (the Santon and Canastel batteries did not have their breechblocks on site);

(*c*) The submarines of the 14th and 18th Flotillas to replace warheads on their torpedoes and to position themselves in the outer harbour between Canastel and the entrance to Oran;

(*d*) Our air squadrons and those of La Senia (local defence bombers and fighters) to be alerted and equipped.'

A good deal of this tactical thinking could be implied or deduced at all levels of the Fleet. 'Amongst the destroyers,' Commandant Pillet said, 'Admiral Gensoul's tactics were understood – to gain as much time as possible in discussion with Captain Holland who had been sent to negotiate and then sail as soon as night fell. Everyone was tense but it was quite plain that the lighting of boilers which caused smoke to be seen from far off had not provoked the English, since they were asking us to join them. But British aircraft had us under constant surveillance and we had difficulty in stopping the gunners from opening fire on them. They contented themselves with shaking their fists.'

Generally a feeling of despair and rage had settled on the fleet after the initial stupefaction. So much had happened to their great country in the last six weeks, so many cherished ideas had been blown into dust – ideas on which decent responsible men had based their lives – that in a sense they met this new situation with a shrug of the shoulders and the wry certainty that anything could now happen but that nothing mattered very much any more.

In the *Strasbourg* no one now wanted to invite Captain Holland on board and, in the flagship, Dufay became the focal point of an almost unbearable curiosity as he sat down to lunch in the wardroom. Putz, who had spent the rest of the forenoon after his return in checking over the damage control arrangements for which he was responsible, recalls that such was the pressure on Dufay who, alone in the *Dunkerque* wardroom, knew what was really going on, that the harassed Flag Lieutenant took to talking in English to his neighbours in order not to give away unwittingly secrets which would soon, alas, be only too clear.

In the British ships out in the bay the same anxieties and doubts, hopes, prayers and fears animated those who had been cast in the role of aggressors. Everyone still believed that in the end it would turn out for the best. The French were bound to see reason. It was unthinkable that they would not want to continue the fight. They detested the Germans as much, if not more than the British. Now that their country had been invaded for the third time in a hundred years, there was all the more reason to continue the fight from overseas as the British would be doing from Canada were Hitler to invade the British Isles. It was common sense.

In the *Hood* Bill Farrell, Somerville's Secretary, and John Rennie, the Secretary to the Chief of Staff, who between them were responsible for the efficiency of the cipher organisation, watched the minutes and the hours go by, aware that the steady stream of signals from the Admiralty showed an increasingly impatient note. The Prime Minister had had to attend that morning's Cabinet meeting without positive news from Mersel-Kebir. The reasonably satisfactory situation report from the other end of the Mediterranean only made matters worse.

'I was told we'd only be away from England for six weeks,' Rennie said. 'Force H was being assembled to sort out the French, I was told. Well, on present form we're not going to do it in a month of Sundays.'

Waiting around with no news from Holland was more difficult for the staff to bear than for those who only had ship's duties to carry out. Staff officers knew what was supposed to take place and were therefore on edge when nothing seemed to be happening at all. They had all been under intense strain since leaving Portsmouth five days ago and Bill Farrell, in particular, was finding it very difficult to live with an Admiral who would never leave things alone. Having been a specialised signal officer the whole of his naval career, Admiral Somerville was already becoming a thorn in the cipher staff's side.

However fast at manipulating numbers they might happen to be, the cipher books of 1940 – in their lead covers so that if thrown overboard in emergency they would sink like stones – were not worked mechanically but by human brains and Farrell had already had to tell his Admiral that the more he interfered, the more the process would be slowed up. They were all working flat out, and just because the Admiral made it his business to be informed by the W/T department as soon as a Most Immediate cipher was received, it helped no one if five minutes later he asked when the plain language version might be expected. With everyone else in the ship sitting around waiting for something to happen, the cipher office was one place where the hum of activity had grown to an almost continuous roar.

Across in the *Ark Royal* similar pressures were being put on his staff by 'Nutty' Wells, the Vice-Admiral, Aircraft Carriers. Here the relationship between staff and ship was further complicated by the fact that *Ark Royal* existed to operate aircraft, and naval airmen were individuals of strong personality whose respect for authority fell a long way short of slavery. 'Give your Admiral an aspirin and tell him to keep out of my way,' was one message not passed on by the Secretary to his Chief, although since the Admiral had a marked though quirkish sense of humour, it might not have been fatal if he had.

In contrast Paymaster Lieutenant Tinniswood, the Captain's Secretary of *Ark Royal*, had spent the morning with comparatively little to do. His Captain 'lay over the ocean' presumably locked in conference with the French. He wondered how he was getting on and thought back on the letter of 'extreme disquiet' which Holland had drafted at Gibraltar and then never sent. Unlike the Admiral, about whom there were mixed feelings on board, his Captain deserved and received a high respect.

He felt a great sympathy for him now, somewhere over there in Mers-el-Kebir. If anyone could pull off the trick, Holland could do it. He knew that, however exhausted Holland might become, he was too wiry to be broken. Again, unlike the Admiral who loved strutting about and keeping everyone on their toes, Tinniswood had never known Holland to lose his temper. He was a very well controlled man – ideal for the job in hand – and Tinniswood wished he could have gone with him on this crucial mission. He was sure it would end in success. And yet . . . and yet the absence of news was disturbing.

'Come on, Sec.,' the Surgeon Commander said, putting his head round the office door, 'Mah Jongg time.'

The Instructor Commander, the two doctors and the Captain's Secretary kept a game of Mah Jongg going in the little-used Senior Officer's Anteroom as and when their other duties allowed them to meet. This was a way of exercising their minds, much as Admiral Somerville kept his brain ticking over on innumerable crosswords in the long periods of waiting.

There was no time for Mah Jongg in the wardroom of HMS *Foxhound* where Holland, Davies and Spearman were having something to eat and drink after their gruelling morning in the motorboat. A guarded optimism, except possibly in Holland's own mind, could still be detected in both officers and men with the sole exception of the R.N.V.R. Sub-Lieutenant who said that, in his opinion, the French would not join us, an opinion which made him seem 'almost a traitor' according to John Hooker, the First Lieutenant. Perhaps nothing underlines the gulf that in reality lay between the British and the French at that time more than this tragically bland assumption on the part of the British that the French must think as they themselves did, and therefore would naturally react as would the English.

Back in London the War Cabinet Secretariat under Sir Edward Bridges and Major General Ismay were writing the Conclusions reached at the 11.30 Cabinet meeting held that morning at 10 Downing Street. The Minute read:

The First Sea Lord informed the War Cabinet of the progress of the operations in regard to the French Fleet. The following were the main points dealt with in the First Sea Lord's statement and in the subsequent discussion:

(1) French ships at Portsmouth had been taken over without

bloodshed. The French sailors had accepted the position cheerfully. Their officers had been sullen and had all said that they would carry out the instructions of their Admiral. It was not clear what those instructions would be, since their Admiral was in London.

(2) A good many of the French sailors at Portsmouth had informed the British officers who were taking over their ships that they wished to become British subjects and to continue the fight on our side. It was suggested in discussion that it might be enough to offer these sailors British citizenship if they served us well and still wished on the conclusion of the war to become British subjects. It was pointed out, however, that this would not safeguard their position, and the general view was that the men's wishes should be granted.

(3) The taking over of the French warships at Plymouth had resulted in a few casualties, the *Surcouf* having offered resistance. One British leading seaman and one French officer had been killed. [In fact one British officer had also been shot dead in the process.]

(4) At Alexandria a definite answer to our demands was expected at twelve noon that day.

(5) The War Cabinet were informed that HMS *Foxhound* had arrived off Oran early that morning, but Captain Holland had reported that the French Admiral had refused to see him. A letter had therefore been handed in, setting out the terms offered. The War Cabinet were reminded that the instructions issued had been that demilitarisation should not figure among the alternatives offered but might be accepted, subject to certain conditions, if volunteered by the French. The question arose whether a signal should now be sent instructing our representative to include among the alternatives offered demilitarisation of the ships to our satisfaction.

The War Cabinet decided: That demilitarisation not having been included in the alternatives first offered, we should not offer it now, as this would look like weakening.

(6) The French had been given a time limit within which to reply, but a written reply was not expected before 11.30 a.m. In the meantime various French warships had furled their awnings, from which it appeared that they might intend to put out to sea.

The War Cabinet decided: That a signal should be sent to Admiral Somerville in the following terms: 'If you consider that the French Fleet are preparing to leave harbour, inform them that if they move, you must open fire.'

The War Cabinet were informed that Admiral Somerville had already been given discretion to lay magnetic mines to prevent the French ships from leaving the harbour.

(7) Later in the meeting, the War Cabinet were informed that a telegram had been received as follows: 'Gensoul's reply refuses our conditions and repeats previous assurances *re* sinking of ships. States he will fight. I am prepared to open fire at 1.30 p.m.'

(8) The War Cabinet were informed that Admiral Darlan had sent instructions to the French Admiral at Dakar calling upon him and his men to pay no attention to British demands and to show themselves worthy of being Frenchmen. It was essential, Admiral Darlan had said, that the fleet at Dakar, with its aircraft component and its full complement of men, should remain under the orders of the French Government.

(9) The attention of the War Cabinet was drawn to Washington telegram No. 1206 which read as follows: 'I showed the President your estimate of the present distribution of the French Fleet and your estimate of the morale of the officers and crew. He volunteered the suggestion that His Majesty's Government might offer to convoy all the French officers and men back to France under a flag of truce, give them a year's pay, delay undertaking to return the ships and equipment to a free France until after the war was over. I asked him whether that meant that American opinion would support forcible seizure of these ships. He said certainly. They would expect them to be seized rather than that they should fall into German hands and he would do everything in his power to help this solution. He said that he had offered to buy the Fleet from the French before the Reynaud Government fell but that there was nobody from whom he could buy it today.'

(10) The War Cabinet were informed that some of the French officers at Portsmouth had asked whether their vessels would continue to fly the Tricolor. The view was expressed that this request ought to be met as far as possible. It was not possible to foresee what forces General de Gaulle would eventually have under his command, but it was possible that these might include a number of warships. On the other hand there were certain vessels in the French Navy which we should need for our own purposes. These vessels might be recommissioned either with a proportion of French seamen or with wholly British crews. The best plan seemed to be to leave the Tricolor flying for the present but not to commit ourselves for the future.

(11) The Secretary of State for Foreign Affairs said that he was drafting a communication to the French Government as to action taken by us in regard to the French Fleet. Its completion might have to wait until there was more definite news from Oran.

122

(1) Agreed that, for the present at any rate, the Tricolor should continue to be flown on the French ships at Portsmouth and Plymouth and that, if need be, the French officers who had inquired on this point should be informed to this effect; but that we should be careful not to enter into any commitments which would make it impossible for us to man some of these vessels with British crews.

(2) Invited the First Lord of the Admiralty to authorise the Admirals at Portsmouth and Plymouth to promise the grant of British nationality to French sailors who volunteered to continue the fight with us.

(3) Invited the Secretary of State for Foreign Affairs to settle, in consultation with the Prime Minister and the First Lord of the Admiralty the terms of a communication to the French Government as to the action taken in regard to the French Fleet. The general line to be taken in this communication would be that we had 'detained' the French ships to prevent them falling into the hands of the enemy.

So much for the cool deliberations of the British War Cabinet at 10 Downing Street. Across in France the main anxiety of coping with the crisis at Mers-el-Kebir was being borne by Admiral Le Luc, stuck in the Post Office of the little Gascon town of Nérac. An hour after receiving Admiral Gensoul's brief warning telegram, the answer came back from Captain Négadelle in the provisional Command Post at the Institution Monange at Clermont-Ferrand that Admiral Darlan could not be contacted. Captain Déramond, another staff officer close to the Admiral of the Fleet, was exploring the suburbs of Vichy in search of suitable headquarter buildings. The experienced Admiral Auphan with the second division of the Admiralty staff was actually on the road between Nérac and Vichy having set off in convoy that very morning, and was thus out of contact and likely so to continue until the evening.

The French Admiralty regulations covering the death or absence of the Commander-in-Chief in war or on operations stipulated that the Chief of Staff should take over in emergency. But what was Le Luc to do? He could consult with no one responsible. He was only too aware of the armistice terms which he had helped to negotiate and which among other things forbade the movement of French warships without prior consultation.

How could he best help Gensoul? What, in such confusion, would be best for France? After turning it over in his mind for nearly two hours, and deciding to delay informing the Germans he despatched the following signal at 1250:

3308 Addressed Admiral Algeria, Admiral Georges Leygues, Admiral Marseilles (Admiral *Dunkerque* for information). *Primo.* I have received the following message. English force comprising 3 battleships, 1 aircraft carrier, cruisers and destroyers off Oran. Ultimatum sent, sink your ships in six hours or we will compel you to do so with force. Answer: French ships will reply to force with force. *Secundo.* Sail in battle order for Oran under the orders of Admiral *Dunkerque.*

At the same time Le Luc ordered the suspension of demobilisation of the naval and Algerian air forces. The aircraft were to be got back into combat condition for service with the Fleet and for a later reprisal attack on Gibraltar.

Since the armistice terms banned the use of radio transmissions from the Admiralty in metropolitan France and since the Germans would immediately have known what was going on had he broadcast this message, Le Luc phoned through the signal on the direct line to Admiralty Marine, Marseilles, with orders to pass it on by cable to Marine Algiers who would then broadcast it from there.

No sooner had he done this than a second signal arrived at Nérac from Gensoul informing the Admiralty of the morning's negotiations in greater detail (but still for some inexplicable reason omitting the Martinique alternative):

Initial English ultimatum was either to sail with the English fleet or destroy ships in six hours to avoid them falling into German or Italian hands. I replied 1° This last hypothesis was not to be envisaged; 2° I shall defend myself with force. At first shot fired against us the whole French Fleet would be lined up against Great Britain, result diametrically opposed to that sought by British government. English reply: If you sail without accepting British propositions which are reasonable and honourable, I shall open fire with regret.

Captain Holland who has served as intermediary has indicated that disarmament of forces at Mers-el-Kebir would be susceptible under proper precautions of giving basis for an arrangement.

Twenty minutes after sending the first general signal rallying the French Fleet to Oran, Le Luc drafted another message, this time personally to Gensoul and not in code:

To Admiral *Dunkerque* from French Admiralty 3309
Tell the British intermediary that the Admiral of the Fleet has given orders for all French forces in the Mediterranean to rally to you immediately. You will then take these forces under your command. Call on submarines and aircraft as necessary. Armistice Commission separately advised.

Le Luc's object in sending this signal in the way he did was to back up Gensoul in the negotiations then thought to be in progress by clearly demonstrating the French will to resist and by bringing pressure to bear on the English by the ordering to sea of fifty French warships.

Unfortunately Fate again stepped in at this point. The message telephoned through to Marseilles at 1330 did not arrive at Mers-el-Kebir until well into the afternoon and by that time the second act of the drama was already under way.

Chapter 9

The noon heat and the human tension at Mers-el-Kebir began to build up in an increasingly oppressive way on the Admiral's bridge of HMS *Hood*.

'Admiral Gensoul confirms former assurances re sinking of ships,' Holland signalled to the Vice-Admiral, Force H, on his return on board *Foxhound*. 'He is determined to fight if force is used. He draws your attention to fact that first round fired will put whole French Navy against us which is opposite of what we want. From activity in ships apparent intention is to put to sea and fight.'

This was to be avoided at all cost. So after a brief conference with his staff, Somerville took the next grim step towards catastrophe and ordered the Vice-Admiral, Aircraft Carriers, to mine the entrance to the harbour of Mers-el-Kebir. This would contain the French Atlantic Fleet. The other ships in Oran itself could be dealt with later, and the mining of the entrance to Oran was not yet ordered.

A few minutes after this order had been given a further signal arrived from *Foxhound*, the intention of which was to alleviate the black hopelessness the previous signal had engendered.

Chief of Staff pointed out preparations made to sink ships at any moment, anywhere and without further orders from French Admiralty. Have passed information re Godfroy to Gensoul.

Perhaps Holland should have come out and discussed the situation with his Admiral. Perhaps Admiral Somerville should have taken the unprecedented risk of getting into his barge and penetrating the harbour itself, to insist on being received in person by the French Commander-in-Chief. Who knows? Per-

Admiral Darlan with Admiral Sir Dudley Pound

The battle-cruiser *Strasbourg*

General view of Mers el Kebir

The French fleet at its moorings

Captain Holland leaving the *Dunkerque*

The bombardment begins

The sinking of the *Bretagne*

The *Mogador*

The *Strasbourg*
starting her escape

The *Strasbourg*
opening fire

The *Dunkerque* after the action

Wreckage on the fore-deck of the *Dunkerque*

Admiral Gensoul

haps the outcome would have been the same. In any event neither of these two actions was taken.

'I had meant to keep *Foxhound* close in to the inner boom,' Holland wrote in his report, 'but Commander Peters pointed out that in this case we should have to run the gauntlet of the shore batteries should hostilities commence, so on the return of the motorboat at 1150, *Foxhound* took up a position outside the outer net boom and within easy V/S touch with *Dunkerque*.'

But the pressure from London via the flagship was increasing. At 1236 Somerville signalled Holland: 'Presume there is now no alternative to ANVIL'; to which Holland replied: 'Your 1236 am afraid not. Am waiting in V/S touch in case acceptance before expiration time. Proposals received 0935.'

ANVIL would be at the end of the road. Once ANVIL was ordered there could be no turning back. Holland therefore tried to delay this dire action to the last possible moment, however agonising the personal tension might be.

'My answer to ask for a final reply before fire was opened,' Holland wrote in his report, 'was based on my appreciation of the French character that an initial refusal will often gradually come round to an acquiescence. I had felt most strongly all along that the use of force, even as a last resource, was fatal to the attainment of our object and I was thus using every endeavour to bring about a peaceful solution. I therefore take full responsibility for any delaying action I may have tried to enforce.'

Thus at 1315, a quarter of an hour before the ultimatum was set to expire and half an hour after the last signals between Vice-Admiral, Force H, and his deputy had been exchanged, Somerville, still in doubt, still hoping against hope that the French would relent, still searching for any valid excuse for delay, signalled Holland: 'Does anything you have said prevent me opening fire?' To this Holland replied: 'Your 1315. Nothing I have said, since terms were not discussed, only handed in and reply received. But I would suggest there might be a chance of avoiding ANVIL if *Foxhound* went in to V/S touch and asked if there was further message before force employed.'

Meanwhile five Swordfish aircraft, escorted by six Skua aircraft, had taken off from the flight deck of *Ark Royal* to mine the entrance to the harbour of Mers-el-Kebir. Two further mines were prepared in case the closing of the separate entrance to Oran itself should also be ordered.

It took about twenty minutes for this mining to be effected. 'At 1330,' Gensoul noted in his report, 'English aircraft dropped four or five mines – probably magnetic – in the channel and the approaches to the channel at Mers-el-Kebir. I ordered Marine Oran to clear the buoys and nets from the southern part of the fairway, sinking the buoys by machine-gun fire, and this was immediately begun.'

Thus, unknown to the British, another escape channel was being prepared. He also brought the Fleet to 30 minutes' notice for steam and ordered them to have full power available on being given the order to sail. The situation already seemed to Gensoul to be *sans issue*, but in his mind the ultimatum would expire at 1500, whereas in Somerville's calculations 1330 was the deadline – and this had already passed. Luckily this misunderstanding did not affect events.

The effect on the watching French of this latest piece of British impertinence, the sealing of their harbour with themselves inside, was to bring their suppressed rage to the boil. Now they were trapped. Whatever blackmail was being imposed on their Admiral, they were all being subjected to a sort of running indignity in that the sky was clearly controlled by the British. No French aircraft were apparent and the British seemed able to do as they pleased.

Indeed, at this moment, over twenty of *Ark Royal*'s aircraft were actually airborne since at 1345 four Swordfish were flown off to relieve the reconnaissance, one to relieve the observation aircraft, two to relieve the anti-submarine patrols and three Skuas to relieve the fighter patrols. Ten minutes later the relieved aircraft began flying back on board the aircraft carrier. In the course of this one Skua force-landed in the sea whilst awaiting its turn, the crew being saved by HMS *Foresight*, an escorting destroyer.

128

Meanwhile the staff in HMS *Hood* were being fed with a continuous stream of intelligence on what was actually going on in the harbours of Oran and Mers-el-Kebir. Just prior to the mining operation, the reconnaissance aircraft reported that the French battleships were sending their float-planes ashore, and that three tugs were *en route* to Mers-el-Kebir from Oran. The boom was opened to let them through and then shut again, no movement of the warships in Mers-el-Kebir yet being observed.

This meant that the Fleet was all but ready to sail, quarter-deck awnings having been furled much earlier in the day. Then at 1342 – after Mers-el-Kebir had been sealed with magnetic mines – four submarines were reported to be leaving Oran, which as yet was open.

Although in fact these submarines were only shifting berth, the move might well presage a major development and Somerville immediately ordered his destroyers to 'proceed to Oran, stop and if necessary sink submarines now leaving'. An anxious twenty minutes ensued. Seven minutes after the order to the destroyers had been given, aircraft reported that, 'No submarines have yet left Oran', and ten minutes after that the British Admiral signalled to the aircraft direct in plain language inquiring if the submarines were in process of leaving. Three minutes later the answer came that they were going alongside a jetty near the entrance.

'Right,' said Somerville, 'then we must stop up that hole as well.' Thereupon he gave the executive order for the entrance to Oran to be mined.

After Somerville and his staff had considered Holland's plea for more time, they decided to take one last chance:

To *Foxhound*. Pass to Gensoul From V.A.(H) If you accept the terms hoist a large square flag at the masthead, otherwise I must open fire at 1500. Your harbour is mined.

This was translated into French and passed to the *Dunkerque*. At about the same time *Ark Royal*'s aircraft reported 'considerable boat activity in Mers-el-Kebir' followed three minutes later by the ominous news that *Dunkerque* and *Strasbourg* have all turrets trained on our battleships. Western *Bretagne* class fore and aft. Eastern *Bretagne* one turret trained.' Another of the reconnaissance aircraft observed some activity on the aerodrome and towards three o'clock, 'Both *Strasbourgs* now have tugs pushing on their port quarters,' which was modified a little later to read, 'Tugs are now pulling sterns to port.'

By this time Gensoul had received the message about hoisting a large square flag if he accepted the propositions. 'The situation seemed to be hopeless,' he later deposed, 'but I was determined that no initiative of mine should provoke the first shot to be fired and I resolved to exhaust all diplomatic resources in order to gain time. With a view to prolonging negotiations I sent the following two signals to the British Admiral via HMS *Foxhound*. 1° at 1415: "I have no intention of sailing. I have telegraphed my Government and am awaiting their reply. Take no irrevocable step"; and 2° at 1430: "Am ready to receive your delegate personally for honourable discussion."'

This was a major move. At last Gensoul and Holland would meet face to face. Things were now happening thick and fast. Gensoul's two signals had just been taken down by *Foxhound* when a further signal came in from the Vice-Admiral, Force H. This was in more peremptory terms: 'Pass to Gensoul. Accept our terms or abandon your ships as I must destroy them at 1530.' Obviously patience was wearing thin on board HMS *Hood*.

Holland did not pass on Somerville's latest ultimatum, perhaps because he felt it would prejudice the negotiations about to take place. Instead he transmitted to the *Hood* Gensoul's agreement to a personal meeting which he had been trying to secure since the early morning.

'I immediately passed this signal to V.A.(H) and made preparations to proceed inshore,' he wrote in his report, 'receiving orders to do so at 1500 and to get an immediate answer. From that moment, until I finally went over the *Dunkerque*'s side, I thought that there was a chance of winning

130

through and that the French Admiral would accept one or other of the proposals.'

Over eight hours had already passed since he had first arrived at Mers-el-Kebir without anything positive to show for it, but for a moment or so hope was renewed and there was a slight *détente*. The hope had a tragic quality but it still remained hope. 'I debated in my mind whether this was merely an excuse to gain time,' Somerville wrote, 'but decided that it was quite possible Admiral Gensoul had only now realised it was my intention to use force if necessary.'

So at 1506, having signalled the French Commander-in-Chief that he was on his way, Captain Holland, accompanied by Lieutenant Commander Davies, once more got into *Foxhound*'s motorboat at a point north of Mers-el-Kebir just clear of the minefield. This involved a passage of seven and a half miles and it was not until over an hour later that he arrived on board *Dunkerque* having transferred to the Commander-in-Chief's barge just inside the net defences of the harbour.

Back in London the atmosphere was grim. Churchill sat all the afternoon in the Cabinet Room 'in frequent contact with my principal colleagues and the First Lord and First Sea Lord . . . the distress of the British Admiral (Somerville) and his principal officers was evident to us from the signals which had passed. At the Admiralty also there was manifest emotion.'

But there could be no weakening of resolve. Desmond Morton, one of Churchill's personal assistants, who was perhaps as close to him as anyone else at this time, kept an eye on what he called 'this complete 18th Century man' that afternoon.

'Winston's real fear that day,' he said, 'was that France would go in with Germany in order to get better terms once the war was over and Germany had won. We none of us knew where we were with Vichy. But that afternoon there were no doubts in Winston's mind as to what had to happen over the French Fleet. He was a very obstinate man and once he had made up his mind, there were no second thoughts. Before coming to a decision he would listen to 'Pug' Ismay (whom he did not particularly like) and to Bridges, who between them ran the War Cabinet, and above all to the First Sea Lord, Dudley Pound, on whom he relied completely for naval advice. But having listened, he then independently made up his mind and on "Catapult" the decision, which was counter to the professional advice he had been given, was completely his own. He was determined to have the French Fleet and if that wasn't possible then no one else would have it.'

It is small wonder that what was then going on at Mers-el-Kebir was later described by Churchill himself as 'Greek tragedy'. The contrast between the British War Cabinet, dominated by Churchill, and the French Vichy Government under Pétain was possibly more marked that afternoon than at any other time in the war.

'Winston was obsessed with morale,' Morton said, 'and, in the intervals of waiting on events, spent part of the afternoon going over a statement he had circulated to the top members of the Government and Civil Service and which he was to read the next day to the House of Commons. It admirably conveys his own mould of thought that anxious afternoon when the drama was unfolding at Mers-el-Kebir and his own inner eye was half on France and half on affairs at home.' The document read:

On what may be the eve of an attempted invasion or battle for our native land, the Prime Minister desires to impress upon all persons holding responsible positions in the Government, in the Fighting Services or in the Civil Departments their duty to maintain a spirit of alert and confident energy. While every precaution must be taken that time and means afford, there are no grounds for supposing that more German troops can be landed in this country, either from the air or across the sea, than can be destroyed or captured by the strong forces at present under arms.

The Royal Air Force is in excellent order and at the highest strength yet attained. The German Navy was never so weak nor the British Army at home so strong as now.

The Prime Minister expects all His Majesty's servants in high places to set an example of steadiness and resolution. They should check and rebuke the expression of loose and ill-digested opinions in their circles, or by their subordinates. They should not hesitate to report, or if necessary remove, any persons, officers or officials who are found to be consciously exercising a disturbing or depressing influence, and whose talk is calculated to spread alarm and despondency. Thus alone will they be worthy of the fighting men who in the air, on the sea and on land, have already met the enemy without any sense of being out-matched in mental qualities.

Across in stricken France there was no one in any position of authority or power who could thus have fired his followers with such a spirit of resistance. The atmosphere was very gloomy in Vichy that afternoon. Towards 2.30 p.m. Le Luc in Nérac succeeded at long last in getting Admiral Darlan on the end of a telephone. He detailed the appalling news. He read out the signals and explained the measures which, very much alone down there in the south-west of France, he had seen fit to take. *'Tout ce que vous avez fait est parfaitement bien fait,'* Darlan curtly replied, approving every action initiated by his Chief of Staff except for reprisals on Gibraltar which, he directed, must wait on his further orders since such a decision would be of high political significance.

An hour later, still stunned and distressed, Darlan informed the Vichy Cabinet of the day's events so far. The Cabinet that afternoon consisted of the aged Marshal Pétain, General Weygand, Monsieur Baudouin in charge of Foreign Affairs, and the rat-like Pierre Laval, whom Darlan distrusted and personally loathed and with whom the only thing he had in common was an antipathy to 'the hereditary enemy'.

The Vichy Cabinet received Darlan's recital of the facts, as he knew them, in shocked silence. No mention was made of the third point in the British ultimatum – the removal of the Fleet to the West Indies – nor could there have been since Gensoul had omitted to pass it on, and it was not until close on 6 p.m. when matters were coming to a head at Mers-el-Kebir that the German Armistice Commission in Wiesbaden was informed of the orders Le Luc had given in the name of the French Admiralty, orders which violated Article 8 of the armistice terms.

Wiesbaden, like Vichy, a quiet resort not far distant from

Frankfurt-am-Main, was where the French and German delegations were daily engaged in hammering out chapter and verse of the armistice signed on 24th June. From about 4.30 p.m. on 3rd July a number of ciphered telegrams began to arrive from Darlan for the French naval commission. Brief though these were, they gave to Vice-Admiral Michelier and to General Huntziger, who was in overall command of the French delegation, a clear picture of what was going on at Mers-el-Kebir.

Like the Government in Vichy both French officers in Wiesbaden were appalled and benumbed. At first sight the effect on the Germans would be incalculable. What would Hitler now do? The Fleet had always been the French Delegation's best bargaining card. This was not sentiment but hard inescapable fact. The French Army had been soundly defeated and lay scattered in pieces all over metropolitan France, but the French Navy until this very moment had been an entity capable of altering the whole course of the war on a single word from its Admiral of the Fleet.

The Germans were well aware of this fact. During the occupation of France not one warship of any size had been allowed to fall into German control. Against great odds and with astonishing daring, the great, not fully completed battlecruisers *Richelieu* and *Jean Bart* had been got away from the Biscay ports to Casablanca and Dakar. Both ships were superior in fighting power to anything the Germans could send to sea.

The French delegation at Wiesbaden were therefore far from being beggars so long as the Fleet remained in being. This was the nub of it all. The Fleet in being. But what was to happen now? As the afternoon wore on, the French delegation decided that the Germans must be told before they found out for themselves but, as at Mers-el-Kebir itself, they decided to delay matters to the last possible moment. Until the first shot was fired, nothing completely irrevocable had taken place, and the definitive meeting between Captain Holland and Admiral Gensoul still lay ahead.

Meanwhile in London towards four o'clock the order to all

French warships in the Mediterranean to rally to Oran and put themselves under Gensoul's command became known to the British Admiralty. Churchill's response was immediate. At 1614 he caused a signal to be sent to Somerville which could scarcely have increased tension in a more dramatic way. The order was direct and to the point: 'Settle matters quickly or you will have reinforcements to deal with.' The strain of the day's evasions and delays had begun to tell and that ominous signal was a stinging reminder of the realities facing them all.

In the harbour of Mers-el-Kebir, whilst Holland and Davies were still *en route* in *Foxhound*'s motorboat, the stage was being finally set. At 1525 aircraft 4K piloted by Lieutenant Everett, R.N., and 4M piloted by Sub-Lieutenant Owensmith, R.N., took off from *Ark Royal* to mine the inner harbour of Oran itself. Both aircraft were Swordfish and in addition to the mines carried an Observer and an Air Gunner in each machine. They flew at 400 feet, reaching the breakwater in twenty minutes. 4K dived over the breakwater, turned towards the entrance and dropped its mine from a height of 150 feet at a distance of 200 yards inside the narrow entrance and in the centre of the channel.

4M, following in line astern, dropped a mine from a height of 150 feet, 200 yards outside the same entrance in the centre of the channel. It appeared that it would be impossible for any ship over 1000 tons to avoid passing over one or the other of these two mines.

Having dropped the mine, 4K flew along the breakwater towards the inner docks at a height of 200 feet. Seventeen destroyers were counted, lying close together in trots, and there was a very large number of transports, auxiliaries, and small craft of every description in the harbour – also a large hospital ship lying beam on to the breakwater. A party of about 50 French sailors in uniform were lounging on the mole. 4K dived upon them to see their reactions and they ran down the breakwater in apparent confusion and alarm. No opposition of any kind was offered, the Pilot stated, during this excursion. Now both Mers-el-Kebir and Oran were sealed.

By this time the British delegation had reached the harbour itself. 'On passing the boom gate vessel,' Holland wrote in his report, 'we were smartly saluted and the crew on deck were called to attention. The Admiral's barge with the Flag Lieutenant on board met us inside the net defences and we transferred to her for the remainder of the journey, leaving the motorboat to await us near the gate vessel. I did not insist on taking in our boat as evidently, from what the Flag Lieutenant said, his Admiral did not wish this.'

Unlike the morning, the relationship between the French Flag Lieutenant and the British Captain was now formal. The intense sympathy and friendship they felt for each other were more present than ever but could not be expressed. Only the eyes revealed what was going on in their hearts and minds. Protocol was politely and correctly observed, Holland and Davies going down into the cabin of the barge whilst Dufay remained '*sur le pont arrière*'.

'Considerable interest was taken in our arrival by all ships in harbour,' Holland went on, 'large numbers of the crews being on the upper deck; in many cases they stood to attention as we passed. Two *Mogador* destroyers had shifted berth since our visit in the morning, one being anchored near the gate entrance and the other under way but returning to her normal berth. All ships were in an advanced state of readiness for sea. All directors and control positions visible were manned and all director rangefinders in tops of battleships, with the exception of the *Strasbourg*, were trained in the direction of our fleet. Tugs were ready by the sterns of each battleship. Guns were trained fore and aft.' The climax was not far off.

But however formal the Flag Lieutenant and the British Captain may have seemed to outside observers on this last leg of the journey, both were suffering personal emotions of a great intensity. Dufay's report makes this very clear:

I must emphasise that I did not fully understand the situation till about 2.30 in the afternoon. The intellectual tension to which I had been subjected throughout the forenoon and my incomplete knowledge of the signals sent and received during my various trips did

136

not allow me to have a clear view of the march of events. But I do think I can make a judgment on the role played by Captain Holland in these circumstances.

I believe this officer forced himself loyally to try and find some common ground for agreement. As proof of this he was at his best when both of us thought we had seen the possibility of an understanding, without daring to be too precise, based on the disarmament of our ships at Mers-el-Kebir.

On the other hand it also seemed to me that, at any rate for a part of the morning, he deceived himself on the extent of the influence he could exercise. I am not speaking of the influence he would have been able to have *vis-à-vis* ourselves by reason of the years he had spent in our country as Naval Attaché, his knowledge of the French language and character as well as the friendly relations he had maintained with numerous French officers.

In my opinion he realised from the start that Admiral Gensoul would never accept the terms of a British ultimatum. But I do think that Captain Holland sought on his own authority a less radical solution in the hope that his personal intervention would get it adopted or at least taken into consideration by his Chiefs (Admiral Somerville, Admiralty, Government). He intended, in fact, to see Admiral Somerville towards midday.

This is why Captain Holland's strictly official attitude at the eleven o'clock meeting [with the Chief of Staff] surprised me but did not strike me as abnormal. As I came back on board, I still believed in the possibility – feeble enough but real – of a deal and I wrongly took the change which had come over the British delegate to mean that he had an understandable wish not to take up negotiations again before he had reported back to his Chief and had obtained from him the wording of an arrangement which could have served as a firm basis for further negotiations.

As it turned out this meeting between himself and his Admiral never took place. Moreover, thanks to his signal projector, he remained in contact with the British forces at sea. His hopes were thus rapidly dashed and I believe that when he came aboard *Dunkerque* at 1600, he had long realised that his role was reduced to that of a simple messenger.

This appreciation I am making on the conduct of the British delegate is based largely on personal impressions but it has a solid grounding of fact. In support of this I will simply cite the following observation – when around 1000 I brought Captain Holland the first reply from the Commander-in-Chief, he talked to me straight away about his role as intermediary and by the words he used then, expressed in barely intelligible English, wracked by emotion and anxiety, I clearly understood that he was not acting under orders but that he had himself asked for this assignment which he had set out to accomplish wearing but a single decoration – the ribbon of the *Légion d'Honneur*.

Such then were the thoughts going through Dufay's mind as the white barge drew alongside the starboard ladder leading to the *Dunkerque*'s quarterdeck. Slowly, and with a stiff dignity, Holland followed by Davies, climbed up the well-scrubbed ladder with its white painted stanchions on to the French quarterdeck which had so often welcomed him in the past and which was so familiar to his tired eyes. All the usual formalities were strictly observed.

'I was piped over the side on arrival and received by the Chief of Staff,' Holland wrote. 'Although large numbers of the crew were on the upper deck, there was a marked lack of officers to be seen both on our arrival and departure. Apart from the Chief of Staff, Flag Lieutenant and Officer of the Watch, I saw only three other officers. We were shown into the Admiral's cabin by the Chief of Staff where we were greeted very formally by Admiral Gensoul. The Chief of Staff remained with us during the discussion.'

Chapter 10

There were in fact five men present at this dramatic encounter which lasted nearly an hour and a half. These were Admiral Gensoul, Captain Danbé, the Chief of Staff, and Lieutenant Dufay on the French side: Captain Holland and Lieutenant Commander Davies on the British. The atmosphere in the cabin was humid and stifling. The ship was partially at Action Stations (thus making it scarcely surprising that Holland saw so few officers standing around on the upper deck) and the scuttles were shut, their deadlights firmly clamped over them, so that the discussion perforce took place in tinned air and by electric light.

Gensoul had spent most of the day, as had Holland, in the open air up on the Admiral's bridge from which he could survey his own fleet and the British fleet at large in the bay and where he was only a few seconds away from his signal staff. It had been hot enough up there on the bridge. Down aft the heat proved to be well nigh unbearable and the high-necked white drill uniform they wore stuck to their bodies like damp clinging sheaths inhibiting their movements and perhaps also dulling their thoughts. The proceedings were conducted in French and once the formalities of greeting were over, it was clear to Holland that the Admiral was extremely angry at the course of events.

'I have only consented to see you at this stage,' he began, 'because I want you, your Admiral and your Government to understand that should the British open fire on us now the first shot fired will not only alienate the whole French Navy but will be tantamount to a declaration of war between France and Great Britain. Is this what you want?'

'Of course not.'

'If your aim is to ensure that the French Fleet will not be used against Great Britain, then force will not achieve this result.' Gensoul's voice rose in tone under the emotion he was feeling. 'You may sink our ships here in Oran but you will then find the whole of the rest of the French Navy actively against you.'

Holland said nothing. He had been prepared for this sort of reception and found it natural that the French Commander-in-Chief should speak his mind with force in his own flagship.

'The sudden arrival of a British Fleet and the presentation of terms which you well know I have no power to accept is an outrage. To face a French Admiral with an ultimatum of this kind, backed up by the laying of mines, is an insult and a disgrace. In any case how can I accept any of the first three clauses of your ultimatum when you have mined the entrances to the harbour?'

Holland waited in silence for the storm of anger to exhaust itself. There was, indeed, no proper answer to the Admiral's last indignant question except, perhaps, to point out that this action had only been taken after many hours of fruitless delay from the British point of view and because it was obvious that the French Fleet would be putting to sea as soon as they were ready and conditions were suitable.

'Your fourth clause,' Gensoul went on, 'I reject out of hand. I have no intention of sinking or abandoning my ships at a moment's notice and I repeat to you here and now what I said a week ago to Admiral North, that I have clear orders, which I shall obey, to sink my ships in order to prevent them falling into German or Italian hands.'

The slight pause which ensued gave Holland the chance of opening a discussion, which he promptly took.

'The British Government is unable to accept those orders as a sufficient guarantee that French warships will not fall into enemy hands and so be used against us,' he said.

The French Admiral stared at him coldly.

'Do you not trust my word of honour?' he asked.

'Of course we trust you,' Holland said quickly, 'as we trust the similar promises made by Admirals Ollive, de Laborde and Estéva. I am quite sure you will do everything possible to prevent your ships falling into enemy hands. However, we do not trust the Germans or the Italians. Both will do all they can by treachery to achieve this end.'

'I am not prepared to listen to that argument.'

Holland fell silent.

'I am the Commander-in-Chief of the Atlantic Fleet,' Gensoul went on, 'and I am perfectly satisfied that whatever may happen to me, adequate measures to sink my ships will be taken.'

'Then let me put it this way, Admiral,' Holland reasoned. 'By sinking your ships you would anyway be breaking the terms of the armistice.'

'Exactly.'

'But should you accept any one of the terms we offered you this morning, you would be acting under *Force Majeure*. The blame for any action, therefore, would be ours.'

It was a plausible argument and in effect was the one which was to save the day at the other end of the Mediterranean as between Godfroy and Cunningham. It was consonant with honour. It offered a pale ray of hope. Neither Gensoul nor Holland had in any way created or caused the situation in which they now found themselves. But the French Admiral was in no mood to clutch at straws.

'So long as Germany and Italy abide by the armistice terms which allow the French Fleet to remain with reduced crews, flying the French flag, in a French metropolitan or colonial port, then I shall do the same, as I am in honour bound to do. Not until Germany or Italy break their promises, shall I break the terms laid down. Those are my orders signed by Admiral Darlan.'

'Admiral Somerville has his orders too.'

'Evidently.'

'The orders given him by the British Government are those contained in the terms you received this morning. Unless those terms are accepted or immediate preparations made to sink your ships, Admiral Somerville will act under those orders and use force. Already and on his own responsibility, my Admiral has disobeyed his orders by not taking action within the time laid down. This, if nothing else, shows his desire to avoid the use of force should this be possible.'

A pause ensued. 'It was at this stage,' Holland wrote in his report, 'that I think Admiral Gensoul began to realise that force might really be used. He produced a secret and personal copy of the orders received from and signed by Admiral Darlan dated 24th June timed 1255.'

The Chief of Staff walked over to the desk and picked up a document which he gave to the Commander-in-Chief. Before passing it over to Holland, who could see that it was heavily stamped '*SECRET ET PERSONNEL*', Gensoul said:

'Before giving you this, I must have your assurance that the contents of this signal will not be disseminated. Should the Germans or Italians know of the existence of these orders, they would take action immediately.'

'I give you my word of honour,' Holland said, and was handed the paper, which he read slowly and carefully under the wary eyes of the French Commander-in-Chief and of his Chief of Staff. On *Flotte de l'Atlantique – Etat-Major* paper and dated *le 24 juin* 1940 the document was headed (in translation):

Extracts from Messages 5143-5144-5145 from the French Admiralty.

The clauses of the Armistice are notified to you *en clair* by other means. I take advantage of these last communications that I can send you in cipher to inform you of my ideas on the subject.

1. Demobilised French warships should remain French under French flag with reduced French crews and berthed in French metropolitan or colonial ports.

2. Secret sabotage precautions should be taken so that neither enemy nor foreigner attempting to take a ship by force would be able to use her.

3. If the Commission interprets the terms of the Armistice other than as shown in paragraph 1 at the moment of executing this new decision, warships should, without other orders, either be taken to the United States of America or scuttled, if it is not possible to do

otherwise, in order to deny them to the enemy. In no case must they be allowed to fall into enemy hands intact.

4. Ships thus taking refuge in foreign lands must not be used in operations of war against Germany or Italy without the orders of C.-in-C. F.M.F. [*Forces Militaires Françaises*].

When Holland had finished reading the signal, he asked the Admiral's permission to make notes. This he was given and he then scribbled out a rough English translation. What Darlan had decreed in his last message before the signing of the armistice came so close to what they were trying to secure by force at that very moment, that Holland felt sickened by the whole affair.

It was now glaringly apparent that the whole of 'Operation Catapult' was an error of judgment and 'ANVIL' – the achieving of the objects of Catapult by force – a tragedy of monumental proportions. But abruptly he stopped this train of thought and directed his attention back to the matter in hand. 'ANVIL' had still not taken place – nor would it so long as he was on board the French flagship – and there might still be a chance of coming to an agreement of some acceptable kind. It was slender, but at least he and the French Commander-in-Chief were face to face and talking to each other. By now the initial anger displayed by Gensoul had lessened into a more normal reserve.

'If we had been aware of this signal,' Holland said, 'it might have changed a lot of things. It's so nearly what we are asking you to do now – to sail to America.'

'Yes,' Gensoul said tersely, 'but not with British crews on board and not under the threat of your guns.'

This was unarguable and Holland knew it. He could not help but see things to a certain extent from the French point of view. To sail the Fleet across the Atlantic or as a last resort to sabotage and sink the ships because the Germans or Italians were about to lay hands on them was one thing, to creep out of their own harbour with reduced crews and British replacements on board, 'convoyed' by a British Fleet, was another.

This to a proud service was a humiliation, an abdication of their sovereign power, and put into question their honour and the whole basis of discipline without which no civilised state and its protective services can exist. Once again with a mental shrug of the shoulders and a sigh, Holland forced himself to continue the argument and persuasive process as best he could. It was getting on for five o'clock.

'The British Government believes that Admiral Darlan is no longer a free agent, and indeed that signal you've just shown me says that the Admiral was seizing the last chance open to him of communicating his orders in secret. That was ten days ago. It seems to back up the argument I put to you this morning through your Flag Lieutenant – namely that Admiral Darlan is no longer in control.'

The three Frenchmen facing him remained completely impassive. Beads of sweat caused by the suffocating heat of the cabin rolled down their foreheads from time to time and in the pause which followed Holland realised he had touched on a very sensitive area. No one then present from either side knew exactly what was happening in metropolitan France.

'I have no reason to suppose Admiral Darlan is no longer the Chief of the Naval Staff,' Gensoul said in the end.

'What reply did you receive to the message you sent your Government this morning? And do you consider it came from Admiral Darlan himself?'

In reality no answer had yet been received, but only the French were aware of this very disturbing fact. The uncertainty and doubt pressing down on Gensoul had, since the morning, enormously increased but this the Admiral contained and kept entirely to himself. He was, after all, a Commander-in-Chief with palatine powers in his own domain, standing in his own cabin aboard his own flagship.

'The answer was to resist by force,' Gensoul said, turning the question in a manner very familiar to Holland from his days as a Naval Attaché. Holland was not convinced, but decided not to press the point at that moment.

'I again stressed to the Commander-in-Chief that Admiral Somerville must obey orders and use force,' Holland continued in his report, 'unless the terms were accepted to our satisfaction immediately. To this Admiral Gensoul reiterated that the first shot fired would alienate our two navies and do untold harm to us and that he would reply to force by force.'

Time was getting very short. Gensoul remained stubborn and would not give way further, except to state that steps had been take to commence the reduction of crews that morning by demobilising a certain number of reservists.

At 1715 an officer entered the Admiral's cabin and gave the Commander-in-Chief a message which he read and then passed over to Holland. It was in French and was from Admiral Somerville out in the bay. 'If one of the British proposals is not accepted by 1730 British Summer Time, repeat 1730 B.S.T. I must sink your ships.'

The area of negotiation was now very reduced. Under high emotion Holland decided to risk one further delaying signal to his own Commander-in-Chief. He wrote out the following message which he showed to the French Admiral who then ordered it be Most Immediately transmitted in plain language to HMS *Hood*.

'To V.A.(H) from Captain Holland via *Foxhound*. Admiral Gensoul says crews being reduced and if threatened by enemy would go Martinique or U.S.A. but this not quite our proposition. Can get no nearer. Signed Holland.'

Whilst this message was being blinked rapidly out to sea, Gensoul, possibly with one eye on history and certainly with a natural desire to keep the record straight, wrote out in his strong cursive hand on *Bâtiment de Ligne Dunkerque* paper the following statement for Holland to give to the British Commander-in-Chief, together with a copy of the French Admiralty messages 5143-5144-5145 of 24th June 1940:

1. The French Fleet must carry out the armistice clauses on account of the consequences which might otherwise arise to Metropolitan France.

2. The Fleet has received strict orders and these orders have been sent to all Commanding Officers so that if after the Armistice the ships are threatened with falling into enemy hands, they would be sent to the U.S.A. or scuttled. See Admiralty message 24/6.

3. These orders will be carried out.

4. Ships at Oran or Mers-el-Kebir have begun since yesterday 2nd July their demobilisation (reduction of crews). Men from North Africa have been disembarked.

It was then 1720. Almost at the very moment Admiral Gensoul finished writing, another officer entered the cabin and gave the Commander-in-Chief a further message. Everyone in the cabin became very still while the Admiral read the signal slowly, carefully and with an agonising immobility of expression. Was this the miracle they were all awaiting? It was long past the eleventh hour. Was there still a chance and was it there on that slip of pink paper which had just been brought into this damp oven of a room?

'At least this will prove to you that we are still in touch with Admiral Darlan,' the French Commander-in-Chief said sadly as he passed over to Holland message 3309 which had left Nérac four hours before. Holland took the piece of paper and read the equivalent of the death sentence with a sinking heart . . . 'Tell the British intermediary that the Admiral of the Fleet has given orders for all French forces in the Mediterranean to rally to you immediately. You will then take these forces under your command. Call on submarines and aircraft as necessary. Armistice Commission separately advised. . . .'

There was no longer any hope and no point in the British intermediary remaining on board the French flagship.

'Our leave-taking was friendly,' Holland wrote in his report, 'and from the Admiral more friendly than our reception. Even at that stage I do not believe he was certain that fire would be opened. Before leaving, I informed the Chief of Staff that should he have anything to communicate he could signal to our boat on board of which was a signalman with a lamp. This was in case Admiral Gensoul finally gave way.

'We left the *Dunkerque* at 1725 and at the same time "Action Stations" was sounded off. Very little effort seemed to be being made to go to Action Stations, and as we passed, large numbers of the crew were still on the upper decks of the battle-ships. The Officer of the Watch on board *Bretagne* saluted

146

smartly as we passed. We transferred to our motorboat at
1735. . . .'

The French Flag Lieutenant accompanied them to this point
and as they saluted each other and said farewell, they were both
unashamedly crying.

Chapter 11

On board HMS *Hood* matters had been brought to a head by
the receipt of Admiralty message 1614/3 which was deciphered
in the flagship by a quarter to five: 'Settle matters quickly or
you will have reinforcements to deal with.' Tempers were brittle
not only in London but also in the bay of Oran, where the British
Fleet had been steaming to and fro like a prowling cat for nearly
eight hours.

Nine minutes later – at 1655 – Somerville passed his final
warning to Gensoul telling him that if the British terms were
not accepted by 1730 fire would be opened. At the same time
he hoisted 'Preparative ANVIL' to Force H. There was no Mah
Jongg being played now on board *Ark Royal* which, for the last
half-hour, had been flying back on board some 25 aircraft, most
of them very short of fuel.

A high state of tension obtained throughout the Fleet. 'Yet
even at this late hour,' John Rennie said, 'we had no doubt it
would still come right. I suppose we were all praying in our
different ways as we waited endlessly closed up at Action
Stations, but right until the very last moment none of us really
believed it would happen.'

The Admiral's Secretary, up with his Admiral on the bridge,
remained convinced that, 'although they had been putting it off
and putting it off, at any moment Gensoul might come over'.
During the afternoon an intelligence report had been received
in HMS *Hood* saying that the Italian Fleet was believed to be
putting to sea. Surely, they all thought, the French would want
to join with their old ally in having a go at the 'ice-creamers' as
they were then contemptuously known? But as the day wore on,
hope ebbed away to a despairingly low level. A decision had
long been inevitable. Now it was imminent.

Captain Holland's last signal to Vice-Admiral, Force H, made from *Dunkerque*, saying that the French Fleet 'if threatened by enemy would go Martinique or U.S.A. but this not quite our proposition, can get no nearer', was received in HMS *Hood* one minute before Somerville's time limit to the French had been set to expire. As this answer 'did not comply with any of the conditions laid down', Somerville wrote in his operation report: 'air striking forces were ordered to fly off and the battleships stood in to the coast'.

But he still held back the order to open fire. This was partly to give the French one final chance and partly to allow Holland to get away. It was also because of a sickening repugnance in himself to the giving of that terrible order. But now the end could only be minutes away. Dusk was upon them and matters would certainly have to be settled before night brought a new situation about.

The British intermediary, in fact, added a complication to the problem. *Foxhound* had been ordered to rejoin the Fleet so as not to be in the line of fire. This caused a lot of heartburn on the bridge. The destroyer's motorboat was inshore waiting to pick up its valuable cargo. Even if Holland got as far as that, the motorboat would then have a long voyage out to sea. If and when the battleships opened fire, they would do so as far away from the French guns as they could conveniently get. In all likelihood, therefore, *Foxhound*'s motorboat would run out of fuel when well at sea and with night falling, as it does in that latitude with an alarming speed, there was a high probability of Captain Holland and the motorboat's crew having to be abandoned and lost.

In the event Somerville delayed the executive order for 'ANVIL' for almost another half-hour. 'We transferred to our motorboat at 1735,' Holland wrote, 'and were clear of the net defences and about one mile to seaward when fire was opened.' But it was a very near thing, and there was still no guarantee of their being picked up.

The departure of Holland and Davies from *Dunkerque* had been witnessed, apart from the Officer of the Watch, the

Admiral and the Chief of Staff, by other officers including Putz, and photographs were taken. Once the barge had set off with the British delegation, Gensoul and Danbé made their way up to the Admiral's bridge of the battleship. As they passed Putz, Gensoul murmured, as if to himself: 'I've done all I can. It's finished. There's nothing more I can do.'

Too much was being asked of the men on the spot. These were sailors, not politicians. 'Whatever might be the future of our arms from then on,' Gensoul wrote in his report, 'I entered this combat with the calm certainty of not having involved my country in a new conflict on my own initiative. Moreover I entered the battle in the least bad conditions possible having delayed the opening of fire. I must also say that, if I believed in not engaging in negotiations with Holland sooner than I did, it was in large measure because I was afraid that if I had gone further this could have brought about a rupture of the armistice which I did not feel qualified to break myself against the advice of the responsible military chiefs and of the government.'

There is an expression, well known to anyone who has served in the Royal Navy, which describes Gensoul's position at that time. He could be said to be 'carrying the can for Their Lordships'. All seagoing naval officers have experience of what this means. Their Lordships in London and Churchill himself may have had a nasty afternoon; those on the spot at Oran were about to risk their lives and in many cases lose them, for a political decision which, to put it mildly, was questionable. But Gensoul was 'carrying the can' for Darlan. He was loyally obeying the orders he had been given. Ironically enough his reward for this stubborn bravery was afterwards to be pointedly cold-shouldered by Darlan, by Weygand and by Pétain himself.

Dufay returned on board *Dunkerque* six minutes before fire was opened. By then French destroyers were under way inside the harbour of Mers-el-Kebir preparatory to breaking out, berthing parties from Oran dockyard were on the mole ready to slip the stern wires of the battleships. The Fleet was at full action stations and all ships were in a state of readiness to sail.

The count-down to what Churchill called 'the deadly stroke' was relentlessly ticking away to zero.

Then it came.

'Fire was opened at maximum visibility range of 17,500 yards at 1754,' Admiral Somerville wrote, 'employing G.I.C. concentration with aircraft spotting. The line of fire was from the north-west, so that fire from the French ships was to some extent blanked by Mers-el-Kebir Fort (Fort Santon) and the risk of damage to civilian life and property reduced.' So the battle began.

To the unwilling aggressors the French Fleet was a sitting duck, return firepower being gravely reduced by the position in the harbour of the four capital ships. But the French had used the long day's delay to advantage. Not only was the Atlantic Fleet itself ready to sail and to fight but the Admiral at Oran had the ships under his command in a similar state of preparedness, the coastal batteries at Santon and Canastel were ready to fire and 42 Fighter aircraft from La Senia had been airborne for thirty minutes.

Moreover, four seaplanes (two from *Dunkerque* and two from *Strasbourg*) had been disembarked since midday, being moored to buoys in the harbour. These all took off from the harbour as soon as the action began and endeavoured to observe the fall of shot of the four French battleships. Finally – and perhaps most important of all – the southern exit channel had been cleared and the Oran minesweepers were in a position ready to sweep the English magnetic mines laid in the approach channels as fire was opened.

Only the bombers at La Senia were incapable of joining in any action over the sea at that time. A few days previously, in spite of strict orders to the contrary, some independently-minded pilots had flown their aircraft to Gibraltar to continue in the war. Since this might well be the thin end of the wedge and was in any case an infraction of the armistice, Colonel Rougevin, who was Commandant of the French Air Forces at La Senia, ordered the remaining bombers to be immobilised by having their tyres let down, their tanks emptied, their propellers sheathed and their batteries removed. So no French bombers appeared.

The aggression at Mers-el-Kebir began when the preparative 'ANVIL' flag was hauled down in the *Hood* and the guns opened fire. The French replied when the signal '*d'appareillage général*' was hauled down in *Dunkerque*, thus making the order to sail executive. Simultaneously the order to open fire was given. Both Admirals then signalled their respective Admiralties by W/T that hostilities had begun. 'Am engaging enemy,' from Somerville, and '*Combat engagé contre forces britanniques*', from Gensoul. The difference in phrasing is a sad irony of the event.

The French destroyers had some 900 metres to go before reaching the harbour mouth. Gensoul had ordered them to precede the *Strasbourg* and *Dunkerque*, which were the most important ships to get out of harbour. Then the older battleships *Bretagne* and *Provence* were to follow and the ancient seaplane carrier *Commandant Teste* was to bring up the rear. The destroyers sailed in the order *Mogador*, *Volta*, *Terrible*, *Lynx*, *Tigre*, and *Kersaint*. The starboard anchor chain of the *Tigre* was discovered to be hopelessly entangled with the port anchor chain of the destroyer next to her. The anchor was therefore let go again, the foc's'le cleared and as the destroyer went full astern the chain ran out faster and faster, whipping along the deck until the ship was free.

The first British salvo of fifteen-inch shells, each one packing over a ton of high explosive, took twenty seconds to arrive and fell short in the sea to the north of the harbour. It raised giant columns of water but did no other damage. Almost immediately further salvoes began enfilading the five French ships along the mole.

The *Strasbourg* had slipped her stern mooring and was already under way. The *Dunkerque* was less lucky. The second salvo to arrive struck the jetty, killing the working party which was preparing to slip the stern mooring of the battleship. The tug on *Dunkerque*'s port quarter was also hit and the tow broken. Now the massacre had really begun and disasters were happening almost simultaneously all over the harbour in the thunder of the guns and the vast columns of water, oil and debris which the British bombardment was raising. By now also the French had opened fire themselves, with surprising accuracy considering the handicaps under which their Gunnery Officers were having to work and the fact that only about half their turrets could bear on the British Fleet because of their position.

Not every British shell exploded. One passed clean between the officer in charge of the stern party of the *Dunkerque* and the men he was addressing. It tore a hole in the deck, a splinter flying up to the nearby *Provence* and killing a spotting officer, the shell itself ending up in the front office of the Police Station at St André on the inshore side of the harbour. Another penetrated the armour of the *Dunkerque* and embedded itself between decks where it was later given a decorative arch by its surprised recipients on which they painted the words: '*Honi soit qui mal y pense*'. But that was much later on.

The main action at Mers-el-Kebir was fought between the *Hood*, *Valiant* and *Resolution* and the four French capital ships *Dunkerque* and *Strasbourg*, *Bretagne* and *Provence*. Had the French Fleet been at sea the firepower of both sides would have been approximately even. The 42,000-ton *Hood* mounted eight 15-inch guns, was 860 feet long and was capable of 32 knots, being designed to reach 25 knots on 2/5ths of her power.

She was a beautiful-looking ship, the epitome of naval design as it had evolved in the year 1916 when she and her sister ships were laid down. In point of fact HMS *Hood* was not completed until 1920 and was the only one of her class ever to go into service. Originally there were to have been four such battle-cruisers under the Emergency War Programme begun in the autumn of 1916 to counterbalance the German battlecruisers of the *Graf Spee* class.

But when the Germans ceased work on all their large ships in 1917, the other three ships of the *Hood* class were abandoned and later dismantled to clear the slipways after the armistice. *Hood* was redesigned to embody the lessons of Jutland, the outstanding feature being the huge areas covered by heavy armour, strong framing, etc.; in fact the general scheme of protection was thought in those days to be 'most comprehensive'. She cost over six million pounds and one thousand three hundred and forty-one officers and men took her to sea and fought the ship. The other two British capital ships were older and slower. HMS *Resolution*, mounting eight 15-inch guns, had been laid down in November 1913 and completed in December 1916 at a cost of £2,500,000. She and HMS *Valiant* were 30,000-ton battleships whose maximum power, even after refitting and modernisation, could not give them much more than 20 knots. But they were very heavily armoured indeed.

The prime target – the two French battlecruisers *Dunkerque* and *Strasbourg* – were newer and faster. Both ships with their 100,000-horsepower Parsons geared turbines were capable of nearly 30 knots. *Dunkerque* had been built at Brest and came into service in April 1937, *Strasbourg* at Penhoet in December 1938. Nearly 700 feet long, they displaced 26,500 tons and with 10,000 tons of armour plate round their control towers, gun turrets and protective decks they were formidable fighting ships.

Both ships had been designed to replace the *France* and *Océan* battlecruisers and had cost 700 million francs which at the rate of exchange prevailing in the late thirties came to some £5-6,000,000. Both ships had two quadruple turrets of 13-inch guns, this grouping having been selected for the pre-war ships of the *Normandie* and *Tourville* classes. The two turrets in each ship were forward of the control tower and were widely separated both to localise effects of shellfire and to reduce blast on the control tower when trained abaft the beam. The ships generally and their bridge structures in particular had been modelled on the British battleship HMS *Nelson*, according to *Jane's Fighting Ships* for 1940, and the percentage of displacement devoted to protection was higher than in any previous capital ship.

The *Provence* and *Bretagne* were very different. Both belonged to the 1912 programme and were already a quarter of a century old when the Second World War had broken out. Both had been designed as coal-burning ships not being converted to oil until

1927. Even their tripod masts and gun directors had only been installed after the First World War. Slow and cumbersome they looked like the antiquities they were but as the result of extensive refitting from 1932 to 1935, they were just able to achieve 20 knots.

They displaced 22,000 tons and their main armament consisted of ten 13-inch guns in five turrets of two guns each. Private naval opinion on the British side regarded them as virtually useless fighting ships and possible death traps in action.

Such then was the disposition as the action began. But the constricted harbour of Mers-el-Kebir and the thousand foot high western hill on which stood Fort Santon put the French at an impossible disadvantage. Within seconds of the first shells falling, the scene was transformed. From calm and orderly preparation, now everything began happening at once.

The *Strasbourg* was away from the jetty and turning towards the harbour mouth. This was achieved in the nick of time. The second or third salvoes from the British battlefleet straddled the position she had just left and would undoubtedly have hit her had she still been there. The roar and crash of guns was deafening and the British shells raised columns of water, oil and wreckage some three hundred feet high, so that anyone in an exposed position was drenched in a black rain, if not struck by flying fragments.

Once a naval action begins the first people who know what is really going on are the spotting officers and ratings in the tops of the battleships who observe the fall of shot and on whose eyes and judgment the success of the bombardment depends. In HMS *Resolution*, the Gunnery Officer, Lt. Commander Eddison, R.N., felt that in spite of the shattering dismay that 'arbitration had degenerated into action', there was a certain relief in the ending of the slow hours of anxiety. All day long he had been at his action station in the spotting top which, in the North African sun, had been like a greenhouse. Moreover, he was dressed in the full anti-flash gear – gloves with gauntlets, a stockinette balaclava to protect the head with a hole in it to accommodate a gas mask should this be necessary, and clean underclothes since, in the days before penicillin and antibiotics, a shell splinter wound was an invitation to gangrene, and gangrene had caused more casualties in the First World War than direct shellfire.

By July 1940 HMS *Resolution* had probably seen more action than any other ship at Mers-el-Kebir. She had been in the assault on Narvik in northern Norway in the spring and had had a bomb on the roof of the aircraft hangar on deck which, luckily, had not penetrated the armour plating. But now a weird effect was being produced as French shells fell among the British ships.

Unlike the British, the French used coloured explosive to assist in spotting accurately a particular turret's fall of shot. So now brilliant reds, blues, yellows and greens seemed to spring up all around them as French shells detonated in the sea, throwing up huge jets of colour like some extraordinary firework display. The French fire was increasingly accurate but as yet no hits had been scored.

The British bombardment lasted exactly ten minutes. So much, though, was happening in Mers-el-Kebir that the sense of time changed and it seemed like hours before the firing eventually ceased. On board the *Dunkerque* the last stern hawser had just been let go and the ship had begun slowly to draw away from the jetty when a shell struck the aircraft hangar and the port upper deck. This caused havoc where it struck and in penetrating below carried away the linkage to the steering gear. A few seconds later a salvo of three 15-inch shells caught the ship and effectively put her out of action. The first of these shells struck one of the gun turrets, the second destroyed some of the ship's main generators so that electric power immediately failed, the third cut through the supply of high-pressure steam in one of the starboard boiler rooms and caused a fire, at the same time destroying the hydraulic machinery controlling the heavily armoured watertight doors. In darkness, therefore, and in appalling conditions of fire, smoke, the screaming of escaping steam and the toxic gases caused by the burning of cordite in the shell hoists, *Dunkerque* was effectively paralysed and drifted slowly into the centre of the harbour, the ship itself sealed up into different compartments which could not communicate with one another.

Moreover, since electric power had failed, the gun control system was impossible to operate. A fatal interruption in range-finding naturally followed and no vital information came from the spotting top to enable the undamaged turret to continue fire.

However, two boiler rooms were still intact, as were the main engines, so the ship was put into hand steering and went slow ahead. The secondary lighting system was brought into operation and fire against HMS *Hood* was resumed. Some forty main armament shells were fired at the British flagship by *Dunkerque*, the last salvoes being seen to straddle her. One hundred and fifty-two anti-aircraft shells were also fired at the British aircraft spotting the fall of shot.

But this valiant attempt to keep going was doomed to failure. *Dunkerque* would never get to sea in the condition she was in, being virtually unmanœuvrable. Gensoul, therefore, ordered the ship to head for the sandy shore at St André on the opposite side of the harbour from the mole. She would then be more under the lee of Santon Fort.

In the early stages of this movement, the *Provence*, the ship alongside *Dunkerque*, opened fire with her five turrets over and across the *Dunkerque*. The close range crash and blast of the *Provence* guns, added to that of their own, made verbal communication on the bridge of *Dunkerque* all but impossible. However *Provence* had slipped her moorings successfully, had turned to port and was beginning to head for the harbour entrance after the *Strasbourg*. Then, a few minutes later, disaster struck this ship as well. She was hit in the stern by a salvo which split her open and also started a serious fire.

A moment or so before the *Provence* caught it, her sister ship the *Bretagne*, still struggling to free herself from the jetty, was also hit in the after part of the ship. This was within about three minutes of fire being opened. An immense column of flame rose to a height of several hundred feet and almost at once she began to sink by the stern.

The fire gained hold at a terrifying speed. Within seven or eight minutes *Bretagne* was ablaze from bridge to quarterdeck. Two minutes later she began slowly to heel over and with a roar and a hissing of steam capsized and sank. Only 300 out of her complement of 1133 escaped with their lives.

'By this time,' Somerville wrote in his report, 'the harbour was clothed in smoke from explosions and fires, rendering direct spotting almost impossible and air spotting most difficult.'

But the British did not have it all their own way. 'Enemy shore batteries,' Somerville went on, 'opened fire about a minute after the first British salvo. These were promptly engaged by *Arethusa* but the range was too great for *Enterprise*'s older guns. Shortly afterwards heavy projectiles commenced to fall near the battleships.'

'The action of the coastal batteries,' Gensoul wrote in his report, 'was remarkably effective, especially that of Santon. This may well have surprised the English who no doubt thought these batteries disarmed.' Some 30 shells were in fact fired by Fort Santon at the *Hood* and a similar number by the Canastel, Gambetta and Espagnole batteries at British destroyers flanking the fleet.

'Enemy fire was at first very short but improved considerably in accuracy,' Somerville went on, 'a number of main armament projectiles (probably 13.4 inch) falling close to all ships and in certain cases straddling. No hits were incurred, but a number of splinters caused minor superficial damage in *Hood* and injuries to one officer and one rating.

'After firing a total of 36 fifteen-inch salvoes, the fire from the French ships died down but fire from the forts was becoming increasingly accurate. Course was altered 180 degrees to port together and ships ordered to make smoke to avoid damage from the fire of the forts.'

Meanwhile, as *Ark Royal*'s aircraft had reported at the start of the action, all six Mers-el-Kebir destroyers were under way, in line ahead, inside the boom but heading for the open sea.

Destroyers with their fine turn of speed are the outriders to a fleet and now, through the noise and the overlying blanket of smoke, as salvo after salvo fell in the harbour, they could be observed speedily getting into a position where they could protect such capital ships as managed to escape.

Their manœuvrability was put to a sudden test as a way was cleared for one of the big ships to go through. This was a great moment in the battle. Heralded by a shout which seemed to ring round the harbour – 'The *Strasbourg* – the *Strasbourg!*' followed by wild cheering, the huge ship could be seen through the swirling smoke, moving with majestic power towards the entrance through the wreckage, the burning oil and the general mess now littering the harbour. It was an inspiring sight. *Strasbourg* was still unscathed. Right from the start she had been too quick for the British rangefinders, their salvoes falling just where the ship had been a few moments before, and indeed, as the French Commander-in-Chief remarked, she would have been hit had she slipped from her berth a single minute later than she did. Now there was a good chance she would escape.

The destroyer *Mogador*, leading ship of the six *Contre Torpilleurs*, was not so lucky. A 15-inch shell caught her just as she was in the channel and on the point of reaching open waters. The projectile struck her near the stern. This provoked an alarming chain reaction. The depth charges aft on the quarterdeck exploded, blowing off the stern of the ship and causing a serious fire.

Almost immediately the ship began to sink by the stern as the fire raged forward. Luckily the main engine room bulkheads held and she was later taken in tow, being beached out of the way in that part of the harbour somewhat inappropriately called the '*Bains la Reine*'.

It took the *Strasbourg* about twenty minutes to clear the harbour and by that time the British bombardment had ceased. Thanks to the smoke her escape was at that juncture unobserved. This feat put renewed heart into the rest of the French Fleet and although her departure was later reported by one of *Ark*

Royal's aircraft at 1818, the fact was not initially believed on board the British flagship.

'Fire on the French ships ceased at 1804,' Somerville wrote. 'My appreciation of the situation at this time was that resistance from the French ships had ceased and that, by ceasing fire, I should give them an opportunity to abandon their ships and thus avoid further loss of life. Since the French knew the entrance to the harbour had been mined, I felt quite positive that no attempt would be made by them to put to sea.

'Force H proceeded to the westward with a view to taking up a position from which further bombardment of the French ships could be carried out if necessary, without causing casualties to men proceeding ashore in boats and without exposing the ships of Force H unduly to the fire of the forts.'

In the event none of the mines laid by the British exploded and a few minutes later *Strasbourg* and her attendant destroyers were out of the harbour and heading east, in other words in a diametrically opposite direction. Captain Collinet's Breton nerve and his brilliant manœuvring of the battlecruiser had paid off.

There was another reason for caution in Somerville's mind. A huge pall of black smoke now lay between Force H and the shore. Whatever was going on behind and beneath that bank of smoke had become invisible to the British at sea as it was also impenetrable to aircraft above it. A couple of hours before the action began Somerville knew that there had been activity at the aerodrome and: 'I now considered it desirable to stand out to seaward to avoid a surprise attack by aircraft under cover of smoke.'

Meanwhile *Strasbourg*, having left the harbour at 15 knots, had quickly worked up to 28 and by about 1820 was abreast the Canastel headland. At this time *Hood* was behind her own smoke screen eight miles to the north-west. For the next ten minutes the two ships, each invisible to the other, drew farther apart. There was thus something like a lull.

Staff opinion on board the *Hood* at this time considered that, although Force H had actually ceased fire quarter of an hour ago, the utter confusion and chaos in the harbour of Mers-el-

Kebir, the incessant aircraft patrols and the continuing fire from their own coastal batteries might have led the French to believe that the action was still in progress.

'Repeated signals,' Somerville wrote, 'were now received from the shore, visual, and wireless stations requesting fire to be ceased, to which the reply was made: "Unless I see your ships sinking, I shall open fire again." '

The situation as it appeared to the French Commander-in-Chief was slightly different as he stood there on the bridge of his crippled battleship. *Strasbourg* and all the destroyers except for the *Mogador* had got away safely and were tearing off east past Canastel and L'Aiguille. Inside the harbour *Bretagne* had been sunk and the *Dunkerque*, *Provence* and *Mogador* were in varying degrees of paralysis. The *Commandant Teste* had been miraculously untouched but this old ship had never been of front-line importance.

'I therefore judged that at least for the moment the English had attained their object,' Gensoul wrote, 'so that I had to make sure, if possible, that they would not again open fire on the disarmed targets our ships had become. I also kept in mind – always provided the English were not going to come back and finish us off – my intention to sail in the course of the night. At that time I knew that *Dunkerque* was incapable of fighting but not of steaming at about 18 knots with two boilers and the main engines working. So I sent the following signals:

1. At 1815 by W/T to Admiral Somerville: 'Ask you to stop firing,' and I also hoisted a square flag at the mainmast. The reason for this was the signal I had received from *Foxhound* at 1410 saying: 'If you accept the propositions, hoist a square flag at the mainmast, otherwise I shall open fire.' In fact, so far as the ships at Mers-el-Kebir were concerned, the English demands had been temporarily satisfied so I therefore had no hesitation in using this signal for some minutes.

2. At 1930 to *Dunkerque*, *Provence* and *Cdt. Teste*: 'At what time will you be ready to sail for Toulon?'

3. In the same spirit at 2130 to Admiral Somerville by W/T: 'Warships at Mers-el-Kebir *hors de combat*. Am evacuating personnel from ships.'

In fact the sophistry in the above does not bear examination even with the refinement of hindsight. This was purely and simply a trick. Gensoul wanted the murder to stop and therefore said to the British: 'We accept your propositions. You have got what you wanted.' There was every humanitarian justification for this. No doubt it is what any responsible officer would have done in similar dire circumstances.

However, the French Admiral had not in fact accepted any propositions whatever. He had had them forced down his throat. Moreover he had no intention whatever of doing anything but evading the British demands. In his mind there was every justification for evasion. He gave the British to understand that his ships were *hors de combat* and that personnel were being evacuated. In view of what subsequently happened, this was to have tragic results.

By this time *Dunkerque* had anchored across the harbour off Port St André and 'towards eight o'clock the Captain of *Dunkerque* informed me of the extent of the damage done and the impossibility of fighting the ship. I ordered him to sink the ship slowly by the bows on the sandy bottom of St André. The operation was executed with the aid of tugs and *Dunkerque* settled gently pointing west in eight metres of water by the bows and thirteen by the stern.'

But this was all later on. At half past six all that Gensoul knew was that *Strasbourg* had got away and that the English had stopped firing at least for the moment. He did all he could to derive some advantage for himself and his Fleet from the disaster. In point of fact, since the signal lockers had been shot away, no square flag could be found and a striped blue counterpane was hoisted as a makeshift signal. 'A white sheet would have given the wrong impression,' Dufay said, who found the necessary emergency flag. 'We were not surrendering, only indicating that the British conditions had been "accepted".'

Elsewhere, notably at Wiesbaden, French wits were also trying to turn the catastrophe to some sort of advantage. Admiral Michelier was in conference with General von Stulpnägel's

Armistice Commission and in particular with the German naval captain Wever, President of the Marine Section.

Wever had been Naval Attaché at Paris and had a high regard for the French Navy. He especially had difficulty in hiding the emotion he felt at the news that the British were at that moment in action against the French Fleet. In diplomatic language he expressed the hope that the losses would not be too great, which only lightly disguised the real sympathy he felt.

The German Delegation also agreed to try to get the Führer's approval for the counter measures ordered by the French Admiralty, which were in technical breach of the armistice terms, and also to try to adjust these terms for the benefit of the French. In this they were successful. Later that night, General Huntziger and Admiral Michelier were informed that Hitler had given his consent to the measures taken and that, until the situation became clearer, the Armistice Commission was ready to suspend those clauses of the armistice which contradicted the action taken by the French Government. In other words, for the time being the French Admiralty retained its sovereignty and such command of the situation as it would normally have had in the circumstances.

Chapter 12

The real action now moved out to sea. In the ten minutes between 1820 and 1830 when *Hood* was behind her own smoke screen a fatal mistake was made, fatal that is to say to the British plan to immobilise or destroy at one blow the entire French Atlantic Fleet. It was this mistake which, in effect, allowed the *Strasbourg* to escape.

'At 1820,' Somerville wrote. 'I received a report from *Ark Royal*'s aircraft that one *Dunkerque* [class battleship] had left harbour and was going east. In view of other reports of movements which had been subsequently cancelled, the difficulty of observation owing to smoke and the certainty I entertained that the French would abandon their ships, I did not attach sufficient weight to this report. It was not until a subsequent report, received at 1830, confirmed the escape of a battlecruiser and destroyers to the eastward [From Aircraft to *Ark Royal* – Total force at present at sea one *Dunkerque* and eight destroyers to East of Oran Bay] that I decided to alter course to the east. The resultant delay, though not appreciably affecting the situation, could have been avoided.' The focus was now on *Ark Royal*. 'Plans had been made to bomb the heavy ships in Mersel-Kebir and the submarines and light craft berthed in Oran harbour,' the Vice-Admiral, Aircraft Carriers, wrote in his report. 'An aircraft torpedo attack on the heavy ships had also been prepared. To launch these attacks when required, and to provide for essential reconnaissance, aircraft spotting, observation, A/S and fighter patrols was a difficult problem of organisation. It could have been done if "ANVIL" had commenced at 1500, but the double postponement to 1757, combined with: (*a*) Provision of two ranges of mines, (*b*) The large number of aircraft which had to be landed on between 1630 and 1800 unless they were to be lost, (c) The approach of the enemy force; combined with the direction of the wind and the approach of darkness, resulted in delays in the despatch of the bomber and torpedo striking forces and the small scale of these attacks.'

A few minutes before the second message from the aircraft patrol arrived, which confirmed that one *Dunkerque* class battleship really was at sea, six Swordfish had been flown off to attack the heavy ships in Mers-el-Kebir. Each of these aircraft carried four 250 lb S.A.P. (Semi Armour Piercing) bombs and eight 20 lb bombs known as 'Coppers' – not exactly a saturation load but capable, if the attack were pressed home with accuracy and determination, of inflicting damage which would slow down the ship.

At the same time three Skuas (monoplane fighters) were flown off to escort the bombers and act as a fighter patrol. Their departure had been delayed by the necessity of landing on a considerable number of other aircraft which had reached the limit of their fuel endurance. This striking force of nine aircraft was now diverted and ordered to attack the battlecruiser which had already got well away to sea.

We took off at 1825, with orders to escort 6 Swordfish proceeding to carry out High Dive Bombing attack on French battleships. Then to return and carry out a Fighter patrol over the ship. About five minutes after taking off 5 French Curtiss 75As were observed, attacking spotting aircraft on starboard quarter of *Ark Royal*. The Section broke up to attack these, and after a short engagement, the French fighters returned to Oran. During the engagement the aircraft flown by Petty Officer Airman T. F. Riddler in Skua L.2915 was observed to spin into the sea. The remaining two Skuas continued to escort the Swordfish.

At about 1910 while at 12,000 feet, 9 French fighters (Curtiss 75As and Morane 406s) were observed above and astern of the Swordfish. A section which appeared to be about to attack them was engaged and a dogfight ensued with all the fighters, during which Sub-Lieutenant (A) G. W. Brokensha in Skua L.2997 obtained some hits on a Curtiss 75 which broke off the engagement. I was able to get a long burst on a Morane, which was on Sub-Lieutenant Brokensha's tail. This aircraft was also steadily engaged by Leading Airman F. Coston (the Observer and Air Gunner in L.2997). Several hits were observed and the machine broke off the combat and dived away.

Several other aircraft were engaged by both Skuas. Three guns on each Skua jammed during this fight.

At about 1930 three Curtisses appeared, and a dogfight ensued with no apparent results on either side. Shortly after this the Swordfish started their attack, and the *Strasbourg* put up a barrage in front of us. We returned towards the carrier. On the way back we met a Berguet *Bizerte* Flying Boat and carried out attacks on it. During my second attack she dropped some bombs on a destroyer. Sub-Lieutenant Brokensha put one engine out of action and observed streams of petrol come out of the tank.

We returned to the carrier and landed on just after sunset.

Before this hazardous return, so economically described, and back in *Ark Royal* the news that *Strasbourg* and her attendant destroyers were at sea, brought with it the instant realisation that the aircraft carrier was in a highly unhealthy position *vis-à-vis* the French battlecruiser. The purpose-built *Ark* could do just over 30 knots. She was a splendid mobile aerodrome but incapable of fighting a battle at sea, and except for sixteen 4.5-inch anti-aircraft guns was defenceless against any bombardment by heavy guns.

Although the great aircraft carrier was already the most famous ship in the Royal Navy, having narrowly missed destruction seven times in the first ten months of the war, there could be no guarantee that her luck would hold for ever. Revolutions for full speed were ordered and she turned away to the north. This brought the Commander (E) up from the Engine Room in his white overalls to complain that these constant alterations in revolutions being rung down from the bridge were making life very difficult in the Engine Room.

In all ships of all kinds the relationship between bridge and engine room hinges on a delicate balance of mutual understanding, the general tenor of complaint from the engine room usually being expressed by: 'If only you'd give us more warning of what you require . . .' In an aircraft carrier when sudden bursts of speed for flying off and flying on aircraft are required, life can indeed be difficult in the engine room and the Commander (E) who had had a bad day was not going to be taken for granted. Unfortunately he had picked on an equally difficult moment on the bridge.

'That's all right, old boy,' the Navigating Officer said in a casual tone of voice, looking down at his chart, 'we've only got the *Strasbourg* after us'. A remark which got the Commander (E) back into the engine room as fast as he could get below.

But the *Strasbourg* herself was not going to be deflected from her escape by any such tempting bait. Captain Collinet knew that he had the *Hood*, with her superior speed and armament to contend with and his object was to get as far away as possible by nightfall so that he could complete his escape during the dark hours.

On leaving Mers-el-Kebir *Strasbourg* had briefly engaged the one destroyer, HMS *Wrestler*, which had been detached from Force H to watch the entrance to the harbour at Oran. By dint of high-speed manœuvring and a measure of luck, the British destroyer avoided being hit but no sooner had *Strasbourg* ceased firing at her than she came under fire from the shore batteries covering Oran. Although ordered by Somerville to withdraw, at least one hundred 4-inch and 6-inch calibre shells fell near her before she got out of range.

'At 1843,' Somerville wrote, 'cruisers and destroyers were ordered to the van. At this time there was some doubt as to how many heavy ships had left harbour, but when it appeared that only one *Dunkerque* was actually at sea, *Hood* and light craft proceeded ahead, leaving the two battleships to follow unscreened.'

Whilst *Hood* steamed at her utmost speed to try and catch up, the bombing attack by the six Swordfish of 818 Squadron took place. Weather conditions were good, the sea calm, and except for a slight haze at sea level visibility was maximum. The attack was made down sun and therefore almost directly from the west so that they came on the battlecruiser from astern in line ahead. This made anti-aircraft fire more difficult and this difficulty was increased by the fact that a splinter had holed

Strasbourg's funnel and she was leaving behind her an involuntary smoke screen.

The Commanding Officer of No. 818 Squadron said that *Strasbourg* was screened by eleven or twelve destroyers of which one was in tow and rapidly dropping astern. The original *Strasbourg* group of destroyers, those who had been with her in Mersel-Kebir and who had sufficient speed to escort her efficiently, had been temporarily joined by other destroyers from Oran to give local support as she passed Cap Canastel. So at the moment of the bombing attack, there were a number of small ships in the vicinity which could in no way protect the *Strasbourg* from a surface attack by the British battleships but which could and did put up an impressive anti-aircraft barrage.

So with the sun just about to set at approximately a quarter to eight in the evening, the six Swordfish in two sections of three dived on the battlecruiser from 11,000 feet to 4,000 feet and at ten-second intervals released their bombs. The French retorted strongly but did not open fire until the first bomb dropped. The British claimed 'one or two probable hits', adding the somewhat rueful comment, based on the reception they were given, that once the bombs were away it was probably better to continue the dive to sea level and skim away a few feet above the surface of the sea rather than pull out of the dive as soon as the bombs were dropped and thus find themselves in a forest of flak.

In fact the approaching aircraft were seen both by Commandant Rosset in the spotting top of *Strasbourg* and by at least one of the French destroyers, *La Poursuivante*, in close support of the battlecruiser. Their joint warnings, given *in extremis* as the French Commander-in-Chief put it, enabled the huge ship to alter course in a matter of seconds and, as she heeled over in a ninety degree turn at twenty-eight knots, she was just able to avoid a 250-lb bomb which exploded in the sea a mere twenty-five metres astern.

Of the nine aircraft which set out on this attack only six returned. One Skua fighter was shot down into the sea and lost together with its pilot, Petty Officer Airman Riddler. Two of the Swordfish biplanes also suffered such damage from French anti-aircraft fire that they crashed into the sea on their way back to *Ark Royal*. However, their crews were picked up by HMS *Wrestler*, who had herself so luckily escaped from the coastal batteries of Oran.

Meanwhile, as Somerville wrote in his report, 'at 1914 a small boat flying a white flag and a white ensign was sighted on the starboard bow [of *Hood*]. *Forester* [another F class destroyer] was ordered to close, and picked up Captain Holland, Lieutenant Commanders Spearman and Davies and the boat's crew. By this time *Hood* was working up to full power with *Arethusa*, *Enterprise* and destroyers in the van.'

Foxhound's sturdy little motorboat which had seen so much hard service that day was abandoned. They were some fifteen miles to seaward off Oran and had been travelling two hours. They were all but out of fuel, and although the sea was still calm, a dark night was upon them and they thus had every prospect of being lost at sea. Therefore when *Forester* tore up to them at 35 knots and then, when almost alongside, went full astern to stop and pick them up, a ragged but heartfelt cheer went up from them all. It had been a long day for the British intermediary, his assistants and the motorboat's crew.

'Between 1933 and 1945,' Somerville went on, 'a French destroyer proceeding west, close to the coast inshore of the Force, was engaged at ranges of 12,000 to 18,000 yards by *Arethusa* and *Enterprise*. *Hood* and later *Valiant* also fired a few main armament salvoes. At least three hits were observed and the destroyer turned back to Oran.'

This was the luckless light cruiser *Rigault de Genouilly*, one of the flotilla under the command of the Admiral at Oran. She had tried to keep up with the *Strasbourg* but had insufficient speed and had turned back to Oran when she was hit. The next day she tried to sail to Algiers but when only six miles off Cape Matifou was sunk by two torpedoes from a British submarine, HMS *Pandora*, which had been patrolling off Algiers throughout the operation.

The only other British submarine, HMS *Proteus*, which had been patrolling off Oran, had been ordered to proceed clear to the northward during the day and was attacked at about this time by the French destroyers *Tigre* and *Lynx*. Two other French destroyers, the *Volta* and *Terrible*, also turned northwards and fired torpedoes at the *Hood*. Due to the long range, however, these were observed approaching and *Hood* altered course away for four minutes to let them go harmlessly past.

By now light was failing fast. Somerville summed up the situation:

All ships proceeded at their utmost speed until 2020 when I decided to abandon the chase. At this time *Strasbourg* and eleven destroyers were reported to be twenty-five miles ahead of *Hood*. From the reports received, I calculated that the Algiers force, which included several 8-inch and 6-inch cruisers and destroyers, would probably meet *Strasbourg* shortly after 2100. I considered that a night contact and engagement under these conditions was not justified. I knew that neither the 13th nor the 8th Destroyer Flotillas had had any recent experience of shadowing and since the French were numerically superior, it appeared to me that the situation could be summed up as follows:

   (i) The prospects of locating and engaging the French battle-cruiser were small;
  (ii) Force H would be at a disadvantage, being silhouetted against the afterglow;
 (iii) The speed of advance was too high to allow the destroyers to spread;
  (iv) The fuel endurance of the 'V' and 'W' class destroyers would not permit of more than three hours' chase;
   (v) Unless *Hood* was in a position to support the advanced forces the latter would be numerically much inferior to the French. This support could not be assured under night action conditions;
  (vi) I did not consider that the possible loss of British ships was justified as against the possibility of French ships being allowed to fall into German or Italian hands;
 (vii) *Valiant* and *Resolution* were unscreened.

Course was accordingly altered to the westward and the Admiralty informed that it was my intention to remain to the westward of Oran during the night and to carry out air attacks on the ships in harbour at dawn or as soon after as possible. I discarded the alternative course of renewing the attack by gunfire owing to the limited endurance of the older destroyers and the greatly increased risk from submarines whilst bombarding.

High-angle fire was opened at intervals on French reconnaissance and bombing aircraft between 1930 and 2100. A few bombs were dropped, but except for four about fifty yards from *Wrestler*, all fell wide. No attacks were pressed home.

The torpedo attack on *Strasbourg* took place twenty minutes after sunset at five minutes to nine. It was to be the last attempt on the ship. The attack was carried out by six Swordfish aircraft carrying torpedoes fitted with Duplex pistols and set to run at a depth of twenty feet. It was well planned and well executed, the aircraft approaching from the land so that the target would be silhouetted against the afterglow. By this time *Hood* and the rest of Force H except for *Ark Royal* had broken off the chase and the slightly eerie conditions of approaching night off a lonely and hostile North African coast made it doubtful if the crew of any aircraft shot down into the sea could be rescued. It was a daring strike.

The initial approach consisted of a search down the coast fifteen miles offshore. As soon as the *Strasbourg* and her attendant destroyers were sighted, the squadron, led by Lieutenant Commander G. B. Hodgkinson, R.N., closed to identify and at once came under long-range A.A. fire for about two minutes. Considering the long range and low angle of sight, this was surprisingly accurate but no aircraft was hit.

The squadron then worked round in a wide sweep ahead and on to the starboard bow of the *Strasbourg* so that they were between the ship and the land. By now the hills of the North African coast were no more than a dark blurred mass and as the squadron flew at about 20 feet above the sea they became invisible to the French. There was a thick haze up to 1000 feet and visibility looking towards the afterglow was about two miles. There was no radar to help either side and both were dependent on the human eye.

When they reached the approximate attacking position, the

aircraft weaved their way up and down under the lee of the coast in a series of loops until the squadron commander judged that the light had dimmed down to a minimum which would enable the target to be adequately silhouetted against the now rapidly fading afterglow. Then they went in.

They came on the ship in two columns of threes, twenty feet above the water and separated one from another by intervals of only three hundred yards. When they reached a suitable position to drop their torpedoes, the section leaders turned to the attack together, their respective sections following in line astern. It was now twenty minutes after sunset and they came unseen until they were almost into the ship. Only two aircraft were fired on by machine-guns from destroyers on the battle-cruiser's starboard side and during the getaway one aircraft was fired on with machine-guns by a group of destroyers seven miles astern of *Strasbourg*.

One torpedo was seen to explode under the stern of the ship and there was some evidence of a hit amidships but darkness and funnel smoke made definite observation all but impossible. No casualties were sustained and none of the six aircraft damaged. They then flew back to *Ark Royal* and at 2310 – two hours later – landed on for the last time that day. Hodgkinson and other of the aircrews had spent over eleven hours in the air since their arrival off Mers-el-Kebir.

'Course was set during the night,' Somerville wrote, 'to reach position 36° 12′ North 1° 48′ West at 0430, 4th July, at which time it was intended to fly off twelve Swordfish and nine Skuas. . . .'

The British were coming back to finish off the job. There was no cheering in *Ark Royal* when these orders were made known.

Chapter 13

Neither was there cheering that night in Mers-el-Kebir. By the time the last British shell had crashed into the harbour such appalling chaos and destruction existed that it generated its own new problems and confusion. No one knew what was really happening nor if the British would open fire again, even though now no more shells were arriving. It might just have been a lull.

Thick black oil covered the harbour and all was dark under the heavy pall of smoke which the evening breeze did little to disperse. A stench of cordite and the raw smell of oil fuel complemented the visual disaster so that the eyes stung and it was at times painful to breathe.

When the *Bretagne* capsized and sank, her mast had come slowly down into the water as if a tall pine tree had been felled. A few men on deck managed to jump clear, others were trapped in the life-saving nets down the ship's sides so that when divers went down later, they found them drowned like a haul of fish caught struggling in the nets but kept under water by the bulk of the ship till they died. Those on the surface of the sea found themselves swimming in oil, half-blind and coughing out the fumes. Rescuers could get no grip on the black slimy arms they were trying to pull out of the water and exhausted men drowned in the oil in front of their eyes. One or two were seized by the hair and kept afloat that way until some grip could be had on their bodies.

The *Commandant Teste*, untouched except for splinters and flying débris, carried out the main rescue operation of those clinging to or swimming beside the hulk which a few minutes before had been a proud battleship of the line. The contrast was extreme. Where else but at sea can you be in the front line at one moment and either drowning or having a hot bath and dressing for dinner the next? But no one dressed for dinner that night at Mers-el-Kebir.

With *Strasbourg* and five of the six destroyers gone, the harbour looked like the half-empty, tattered battlefield it was when eventually the smoke dispersed. The lighthouse at the end of the mole had been pulverised. On the other side of the harbour *Dunkerque* lay aground bows on to St André, *Provence* roughly a thousand metres to the south-east was beached head on to Roseville and the little destroyer *Mogador*, with no stern on her, was similarly *hors de combat* at Bains la Reine. Only the *Commandant Teste* was left, moored where she always had been, at the mole across that harbour so weirdly littered with grotesque pieces of wreckage and with desperate men struggling in the oily filth.

Of the four seaplanes from *Dunkerque* and *Strasbourg* which had taken off from the harbour at the start of the action, one had been badly struck by anti-aircraft fire and had managed to reach Arzew at nightfall, the second put down in the sea for ten minutes to shake off a British fighter and then took off again to shadow Force H, returning later to Mers-el-Kebir. The third contrived to signal all the movements of the British Fleet in spite of intense high-angle fire from the ships, some of it from the departing *Strasbourg*. This aircraft was attacked in the air by the British and also accidentally by one French fighter, but succeeded in reaching Mostaganem for the night. The fourth also shadowed the British Fleet and reported that *Hood* had broken off the chase at 2025. After attacks similar to the others, this aircraft finally landed at Arzew for the night.

In the stricken flagship they were trying to restore electric power, put out the fires and assess the real extent of the damage, most of which appeared to be amidships. *Enseigne de Vaisseau* Putz, who had been in the thick of it from the start, repaired to the wardroom at a late hour to find it turned into a sort of cafeteria where exhausted officers, half intoxicated by the fumes, were trying to quench their ravening thirst with an excess of wine and beer. There was intense bitterness against the British and all of them were suffering from varying degrees of shock and exposure.

All had seen sights and had experiences in the past few hours of an awe-inspiring enormity. 'In the first few minutes of the action,' Putz said, 'I remember a Petty Officer asking me where the nearest first aid station was. He was dazed and had been wounded in the face which he had covered with his hands but he was able to stagger in the direction I told him. Later on, when I asked the surgeon what had happened to him, he said he reached the sick bay but died on arrival, the whole of his exposed skin having been burnt off.'

Nerves had been stretched to and in some cases beyond breaking point. Everyone was intoxicated, in the real meaning of the word, by the foul air they had been forced to breathe since disaster had struck the ship. There seemed to be no escape from this stench. Each compartment they opened up released further clouds of nauseous fumes, the mixture of oil, smoke and dead human bodies, some of them barbecued out of recognition, being almost impossible to endure. Yet they had to endure it.

Appalling things had happened. The second salvo to hit the ship had pierced one of the boiler rooms, killing every stoker with the escape of high pressure steam. It had also cut the main electricity supply so that the task of opening up these compartments in darkness and getting out the bodies required an almost superhuman nerve and courage. When the tally was made, in *Dunkerque* alone, some five officers and one hundred and thirty men had been killed outright and another fifty wounded, although the bodies of two stokers were not found till about a month later when eventually a passage was cleared and they were discovered in a state of decomposition where they had crawled in a pathetic attempt to escape the fire and high pressure steam.

The French Commander-in-Chief reported to Darlan on the day's work:

The comparison between French and British losses in the course of this action is cruelly to our disadvantage. But our unexpected enemies cannot flatter themselves, as they had hoped, on having wiped out the entire Fleet in this trap of Mers-el-Kebir.

The calm bearing of all personnel under a bombardment of extreme violence, the skilful manœuvring of Commanding Officers and staffs whose ships were not seriously damaged at the start of the battle, the fighting spirit of ships' companies which I observed myself and have had reported to me, assure me that in a less treacherous action, our Fleet would have fought with distinction and advantage.

I must finally remark – since it is a proof of morale which events have never before put to the test – on the numerous individual and collective witnesses who have assured me that your orders and my orders not to submit to force and to answer force with force were understood and obeyed without any hesitation and without counting the cost.

Admiral Gensoul took his staff ashore during the night and established himself in Oran. Later he ordered the ship to be evacuated, its anti-aircraft defence being undertaken by shore batteries.

This certainly did not go down well with the ship's officers who were unwilling to leave the ship (though in no way sorry to see the staff depart) and before the order was brought into force anti-aircraft gun crews remained at their action stations, sleeping where they could around their guns, so that they would be instantly ready to give the British a hot welcome should a return visit be made.

In spite of the dreadful mess they were having to clear up, morale remained good, fired as it was by indignation and anger. This morale was undoubtedly helped by *le grand Pierre*, 'Tanguy-Tanguy', or 'Merde-merde', the *Dunkerque's* exceptional Commander who knew every single one of the twelve hundred strong ship's company by name – a rare feat of memory indeed.

No one relaxed but they all dropped into the wardroom from time to time for a break. Order gradually and methodically restored itself as each area of disaster was investigated and assessed. Work on a coffer dam was begun so that the ship could repair herself without sinking in the process. Electric power was partially restored and throughout the long black night, the bodies of their dead shipmates were brought up on deck and covered over until they could be identified and later buried.

'There were some weird contrasts, though, arising from the action,' Putz said, 'which came back to mind as we worked. For instance the shell which struck No. 2 turret broke off some armour plating which acted as a sort of giant piston and crushed everyone in the turret to death. In No. 1 turret there was no knowledge of this and this turret continued through the action undamaged. Therefore, when we all stood down from action stations, the crew of No. 1 turret behaved as they had normally been trained to do. They left the turret at a smart double, arms bent at the elbows and in to the sides as if on parade. It was fantastic to see them run out of the turret in this way, as if being inspected by an Admiral, while only a few feet away lay the dead bodies of their comrades mangled in a crazy mass of twisted steel. . . .'

So the night wore on. It was all but incredible to remember that less than twelve hours ago this had been a highly organised naval township with all its functions specified and distinct. By this same time the day before they had all read the daily orders for the coming day, they knew which was the duty watch, who was manning the anti-aircraft guns, cleaning the ship or going ashore on leave. Now, with the bulk of the ship's company getting what rest they could forward on deck or below, with the bows of the ship on the soft sand of St André, with one of her huge turrets wrecked and with a gaping hole in her side, the mighty ship – their ship – lay crippled waiting for the dawn and the possible return of the British. . . .

Meanwhile *Strasbourg* pressed on through the night. She had kept along the coast past the Cap de l'Aiguille towards Algiers from which port four mixed divisions of ships, having sailed at 1630 had been ordered to rendezvous with her at a point set by the Admiral at Marseilles. At 2115, however, an accident occurred in one of *Strasbourg*'s boiler rooms. Five stokers died as a result of this and speed had to be reduced to 20 knots.

It was not until three-quarters of an hour had passed that

the ship was again able to reach 25 knots but, as she could no longer make the rendezvous, she turned north alone except for the three destroyers *Volta*, *Terrible* and *Tigre* which had the speed to keep up with her. Fearing a possible encounter with Force H, she avoided the Minorcan narrows and instead rounded the southern tip of Sardinia, setting course as directly as possible for Toulon.

On board *Ark Royal* work went on through the night refuelling and re-arming aircraft for the day ahead. 'By 2310,' Vice-Admiral, Aircraft Carriers reported, 'all torpedo aircraft had been flown back on board. Course was altered to pass astern of Force H and to reach position 36° 12' N. 1° 48' W. at 0430 next morning in readiness to launch air striking forces to attack French battlecruiser in Mers-el-Kebir at dawn.'

But nothing is ever certain at sea. At one o'clock in the morning the British Fleet ran into fog and for safety's sake *Ark Royal* ordered her destroyers to keep astern of her in case she accidentally ran one of them down in the night. An hour later visibility improved and at 0330 *Ark Royal* sighted *Hood* and altered course to 060°. Fifty minutes later the destroyers resumed their positions on the screen and as dawn approached it looked as though everything was set for yet another hateful and hated attack. Yet if the job had to be done at all, it needed to be effectively carried out, with as much economy in lives and material as could be managed.

'At 0430,' Admiral Wells wrote, 'twelve Swordfish each armed with six 250 lb S.A.P. bombs were ready to take off to attack French battlecruiser reported by aircraft previous evening to have been beached under Fort Mers-el-Kebir. It was intended that this striking force should be immediately followed by a second, composed of nine Skuas with one 500 lb S.A.P. bomb each for dive bombing attack on the same ship.'

The intention, in other words, was for the first wave of bombers to open up the ship and silence any opposition she might be able to put up and for the second larger bombs to finish her off and make certain she sank where she was, to remain unusable till the end of the war or perhaps for ever.

178

But *Ark Royal*'s aircraft would still have the shore anti-aircraft barrage to contend with and a successful attack on the *Dunkerque* in such a well-defended position relied upon surprise before full daylight would alter the odds.

'Unfortunately *Ark Royal* ran into thick fog at 0420,' the Admiral continued, 'which persisted until after 0600.'

The Vice-Admiral, Aircraft Carriers, therefore abandoned the attack and reported this decision to the Senior Officer, Force H. At 0620 *Ark Royal* sighted Force H bearing 180°, course and speed being adjusted to take station in the line.

In view of this enforced change of plan, 'and also of a message I had received from Admiral Gensoul stating that his ships were *hors de combat* and that he was ordering personnel to evacuate their ships,' Somerville wrote, 'I shaped course for Gibraltar, all ships being secured alongside by 1900, 4th July.'

At much the same time the *Strasbourg* with her three destroyers entered the harbour of Toulon as dusk was falling on what might be described as the first of the interim days. This heroic arrival was greeted by wild acclamation not only from every ship in Toulon but also it seemed by the entire population of the only big naval port left in French hands in metropolitan France.

Now there was to be a pause. Both sides took stock of the situation at all levels, wrote their various reports, succoured the wounded and set about burying the dead. Throughout the long night at Mers-el-Kebir the little boats had come and gone in the harbour taking the dead and the wounded ashore or to the hospital ship in Oran.

As the long hours passed these sorry fires started by the British bombardment still glowed opaquely through the dark foggy haze. Exhausted officers and men, their feelings bruised beyond anything they had previously endured, fell into a deep sleep wherever they happened to be. But the accidental mercy of the fog at sea was only to grant them a temporary respite. Another horror was yet to come.

Chapter 14

The repercussions began. 'War Cabinet 193(40). Conclusions of a Meeting of the War Cabinet held at 10 Downing Street s.w.1 on Thursday, July 4, 1940 at 11.30 a.m. Present: The Right Hon. Winston S. Churchill, M.P., Prime Minister; the Right Hon. Neville Chamberlain, M.P., Lord President of the Council; the Right Hon. C. R. Attlee, M.P., Lord Privy Seal; the Right Hon. A. Greenwood, M.P., Minister without Portfolio; the Right Hon. Viscount Halifax, Secretary of State for Foreign Affairs, etc., etc., etc.'

They were all there. The First Lord, the First Sea Lord, the Secretary of State for War, the Chief of the Imperial General Staff. In all, seventeen high officers of State and five secretaries sat down to hear:

. . . particulars of the operations undertaken on the previous day against French warships at Oran and as to the present position at Alexandria . . . reference was made to the extent to which reports of the operations at Oran had already been broadcast or had appeared in the Press. It was important that we should get in first with our account of the action.

The Minister of Information said that an account of the action, presenting the British measures in a favourable light, had been telegraphed to the United States press by Mr Knickerbocker.

The Secretary of State for Foreign Affairs said that both M. Corbin, the former French Ambassador, and M. Cambon, the French Chargé d'Affaires, had called at the Foreign Office to protest against our action in regard to the French warships at Portsmouth and Plymouth. We must, of course, expect much sharper protests when the news of the operations at Oran were known.

The Prime Minister indicated the main lines of the statement which he proposed to make in the House of Commons that afternoon. A suggestion that we might offer compensation to the dependents of

French personnel who had become casualties in the action off Oran was not approved, as being likely to be misinterpreted. . . .

Then the Chief of the Naval Staff got down to detail as the partial failure of the operation at Mers-el-Kebir became apparent.

The French battlecruiser *Dunkerque* which had escaped undamaged from Oran [getting the name of the ship wrong] had been subsequently attacked by torpedo bombers which had claimed one hit, thereby reducing the speed of the ship [which again was not true]. In reply to an Admiralty signal ordering him to engage this battlecruiser, Admiral Somerville had replied he was unable to do so and that, in view of the situation, he was withdrawing westwards and would send a full report on arrival at Gibraltar.

It was not a satisfactory conclusion, whatever the Prime Minister was going to say in the House that afternoon or however favourable a light Mr Knickerbocker might shine on the matter.

A signal had been received early that morning that weather conditions were unsuitable for an air attack on ships at Oran and that Admiral Somerville was on his way back to Gibraltar. He was expected to arrive there about 4 p.m. that afternoon. No reports had yet been received of the damage sustained by our own forces, but in view of the fact that they had spent the night cruising about at 16 knots, serious damage could not have been inflicted. No encounters had been made with the French Naval Forces despatched from Toulon and Algiers.

They could all read between the lines and, though no criticism of the original decision is on record (except from those who were ordered to carry it out), it was impossible to listen to this recital of the facts without considerable misgiving.

The position at Alexandria remained unsatisfactory, since, on receipt of the news from Oran, Admiral Godfroy had declined to continue negotiations and had discontinued the process of discharging oil fuel.

This was scarcely surprising and there was certainly no comfort to be had from the eastern end of the Mediterranean.

Was any advantage whatever going to accrue from the dreadful action which had been taken?

Admiral Cunningham had been faced with three alternatives: (*a*) To send boarding parties to capture the ships; (*b*) To sink the ships at their moorings; (*c*) To demand that Admiral Godfroy should either surrender his ships or submit them to internment; failing which the ships would be sunk.

Admiral Cunningham had rejected courses (*a*) and (*b*) as the French Forces would be on the alert and the sinking of the French ships at their moorings would interfere with traffic in the port and would probably result in a battle in Alexandria harbour. It was of vital importance to avoid such a battle . . . we were not in a position at Alexandria to take the strong line of action that we had taken at Oran. . . .

The sombre recital of the snags went on. When it was over the Prime Minister said: 'a quick solution of the problem must be reached. It was most important for the Eastern Mediterranean Fleet to regain its mobility and the spectacle of a deadlock in the harbour would do great harm to Egyptian opinion.' For these reasons he deprecated the suggestion to starve out the French Forces.

Egyptian opinion was one thing, what the deadlock was doing to world opinion another. There is no doubt that on 4th July 1940 England was very much alone.

At the same time as the British War Cabinet was meeting in London, Vice-Admiral Michelier had gone to the Nassauer Hof in Wiesbaden. This was the Headquarters of the German Armistice Commission and the Admiral was ushered into Captain Wever's room without delay. He found Wever 'in an extraordinary state of emotion', expressing his personal sympathy for the 'painful situation' caused by the previous day's action at Oran and more especially for the loss of the *Bretagne* and her ship's company.

Having thanked him, the Admiral pressed home the points he intended to make. The English attack, he said, created a new situation which had a considerable bearing on the way the naval clauses of the armistice were to be applied. As a result of this, the French delegation was now asking for: (1) A pure and simple suspension of Article 8 of the armistice terms; (2) The immediate release of 575 officers and civil servants of the Ministry of Marine who were under detention at Rochefort together with their archives; (3) Free passage to Gibraltar of warships and merchant ships which had been forbidden by the German Armistice Commission on 30th June.

Admiral Michelier was a shrewd negotiator. To take maximum advantage of the situation, he was wise enough not to ask for too much. But the practical effect of these demands, should they be granted, would be to cancel out the principal restrictive conditions imposed on the French Navy. More especially it would halt the demobilisation of naval personnel and the disarming of warships.

Captain Wever accepted all three requests and promised to send them on at once to Berlin. Some two hours later Admiral Michelier was again summoned to the Nassauer Hof to hear Hitler's reply. This proved to be a straight granting of all three requests and the added rider that orders to this effect had already been given by the German High Command. Such an unexpected success was received in Vichy with surprise and relief. At least something of benefit to France had come out of the British attack.

Meanwhile Admiral Somerville, *en route* to Gibraltar, was drafting his Report of Proceedings and considering the previous day's events in depth:

Although it is somewhat outside the scope of this report, it is, perhaps, not out of place to speculate whether the use of force might not have been avoided had Admiral Gensoul agreed to meet Captain Holland in the first instance. The final offer made by the French Admiral was very near to a British alternative but differed, unfortunately, in the proviso that the action proposed would not be carried into effect *unless* there was a danger of the French ships falling into the hands of the enemy.

Admiral Gensoul claimed that this danger was not imminent; we maintained that it was. I believe that given more time Captain Holland might have succeeded in converting Admiral Gensoul to our point of view. At the actual time when the French Admiral

183

made his offer it was already too late, since French reinforcements were approaching and the orders of His Majesty's Government were explicit that a decision had to be reached before dark.

I consider that Captain C. S. Holland carried out his most difficult task with the greatest tact, courage and perseverance. That he failed in his mission was not his fault, that he so nearly succeeded is greatly to his credit.

The British intermediary was waiting on the jetty when *Foxhound* secured alongside, one of the last destroyers to get in to Gibraltar on the evening of 4th July. Captain Holland had reverted to his proper role of Commanding Officer, HMS *Ark Royal*, and at first Commander Peters, the Captain of *Foxhound*, did not connect the figure waiting for a gangway to be placed with his guest of the previous two days. For all he knew Captain Holland and his motorboat's crew had been left behind at Oran or lost at sea. But now the first person to step on board was Holland himself, followed by his steward with a case of champagne.

'I wanted to thank you personally for your hospitality,' Holland said, 'and I'm extremely sorry I lost you your motorboat.'

But there was to be no time for the drinking of champagne and certainly no victory to celebrate. All ships of Force H were at once ordered to complete with fuel and ammunition and be ready to sail by 0530 the following day, with the equally grim prospect of carrying out similar operations against the *Richelieu* at Dakar should these be ordered.

Now that they were in harbour and there was no necessity for W/T silence, an almost incessant dialogue began between the Admiralty and the Vice-Admiral, Force H. What were the facts? What was the extent of the damage to *Dunkerque*? Was it Somerville's opinion that she could not be refloated and brought back into service in less than a year?

The questions were immediate and of vital importance. But how could a certain and satisfactory answer possibly be given?

'At 2240, in reply to Admiralty message 1929/4th July,' Somerville wrote in his Report of Proceedings, 'I informed the

Admiralty that from aircraft observation it was not possible to state the extent to which *Dunkerque* had been damaged in Mersel-Kebir harbour, but that she was definitely aground.'

The strategic decision on the next disagreeable chore to be given to Force H was further bedevilled by a matter which the First Sea Lord had brought up that morning at the Cabinet meeting. What action was the Royal Navy now to take should they encounter units of the French Fleet at sea? The Vichy Government had issued orders that all British ships and aircraft were forbidden to approach within twenty sea miles of any French harbours under penalty of being fired on without warning. Was it our intention, he asked, to impose a similar twenty-mile limit and should all French Naval Forces now be assumed as hostile and be engaged at sight?

'After some discussion,' the Cabinet minutes reveal, 'the view was taken that the course to be adopted in all circumstances where the available British Forces were considered strong enough, should be the same as that adopted at Oran. It was still our object to prevent units of the French Fleet falling into German hands and to do so, if possible, without bloodshed.'

This was the Establishment as its 'woolliest'. In other words, if we were strong enough we were to wave a big stick; otherwise, no doubt, it would be wiser to evade the issue.

That morning's meeting had ended with the Cabinet taking note of the above statements and agreeing that:

when French naval forces were encountered on the high seas, the course of action to be adopted should be as follows:
(1) Signal to heave-to;
(2) Offer the ships the same terms as were offered to the French Admiral at Oran;
(3) If the signal to 'heave-to' or the terms offered were not complied with, action should be taken to obtain possession of the ships or, if necessary, to sink them.

They further agreed that instructions should be sent to the Commanders of defended ports on the lines above but subject to such modification as might be necessary.

Within hours they were overtaken by events. The submarine

185

HMS *Pandora* on patrol off Algiers sank without warning a French light cruiser. Now the fat was in the fire. It would not take very much more for the French to declare war on the British. Again this event took place because of a lack of communication – because the submarines concerned were continuing to act under the orders they had been given for 'Operation Catapult' – and no one had told them to stop.

'At 1358 GMT on the 4th July,' the Captain of the submarine reported, 'I sighted a cruiser of the *La Galissionère* class. I turned at once to a firing course and ran in as long as possible. Four torpedoes were fired at 1407 on a 120 degrees track at an estimated range of 3,800 yards. Certainly two and probably three hits were obtained and the cruiser stopped at once and very soon became very heavily on fire. I closed to see if there was any chance of the ship being saved and having decided that there was not, I altered course away. At 1522 the ship sank by the stern and a few seconds later there was an extremely heavy explosion, presumably the after magazines.'

This could not have happened at a more delicate time. The Admiralty were in process of getting out instructions to implement the Cabinet decision that morning as to the attitude to be adopted by HM Ships towards French warships. These were passed to Gibraltar in a signal whose time of origin was 2005/4th July and Admiral Somerville received a copy of this during the following forenoon, i.e. Friday, 5th July. Almost simultaneously he received the report from *Pandora* that she had sunk a French ship. So what now? Were these new instructions to be complied with by the submarines operating off Algiers and Oran? Up to now they had been under orders for the ill-fated 'Operation Catapult'. Yes, said the Admiralty, they were certainly to obey the new instructions and this news was passed to the two submarines at about nine o'clock that night. By then it was a little late. 'Catapult', as Admiral North had forecast, had already become 'Boomerang'.

'Between 0100 and 0200 on the 5th July,' Somerville wrote, 'unidentified aircraft dropped bombs and what were reported to be mines in the approaches to Gibraltar. Action was immediately taken by the Admiral Commanding, North Atlantic Station (Admiral North), to have the approaches swept by Double "L" and Oropesa sweeps.'

This air attack might be simply a natural retort by the French to the aggression done them two days before or it might herald a subsequent declaration of war. It was impossible to know at Gibraltar. However, a significant order, not at that time known to the British, had been given by Darlan late on the Wednesday night with *Strasbourg en route* to Toulon and Gensoul evacuating his ships at Mers-el-Kebir. This order placed the French Atlantic Fleet under the command of Admiral Estéva at Bizerta. The reason for this was not immediately apparent and it had one deadly consequence.

'The next day, the 4th July,' Admiral Gensoul said, 'Admiral Estéva in his new capacity as Commander-in-Chief sent out an information signal from Bizerta detailing the events at Mers-el-Kebir and containing the unfortunate sentence: 'The damage to *Dunkerque* is minimal and the ship will soon be repaired!'

When Gensoul was given this signal at his temporary headquarters in Oran, Dufay says he had never seen him more angry. And with every justification. He knew what such an irresponsible action was bound to provoke – another attack by the British. It was an open invitation to come back and finish off the job. It is incredible that this did not also occur to Admiral Estéva himself.

Thus during the night of 4th/5th July at 0308 (Force H being ready to sail at 0530): 'I received Admiralty message 0056/5th July,' Somerville wrote, 'stating that unless I was certain that *Dunkerque* could not be refloated and repaired in less than a year, she should be subjected to further destruction by bombardment on 6th July, and this was to take precedence over the operation against *Richelieu*.'

Accordingly the dawn sailing was cancelled and plans for another attack on the *Dunkerque* prepared at a feverish pace. 'At 1329 I informed the Admiralty that I intended using *Hood, Valiant, Ark Royal, Arethusa, Enterprise* and ten destroyers for further operations against *Dunkerque* and that bombardment was expected to commence at 0900 the following morning (Saturday, 6th July).'

So the staff got down to the detailed orders for 'Operation Lever'. At first sight it may seem a comparatively simple matter for powerful, self-contained units such as cruisers, battleships and battlecruisers to combine together in a fleet, put to sea and go into action. It is not like that at all. Substantial amounts of intelligence of every kind have to be sifted and digested. Calculations based on fuel endurance of each ship must be checked and rechecked against every foreseeable eventuality. It is no good sending a slow battleship into hostile waters if, for instance, her destroyer screen is liable to run out of fuel. There were other problems in linking a fast battlecruiser to a slow battleship. What air support could be provided? What submarine and air opposition was to be expected?

Time had been so short for getting out the original orders for 'Catapult' that in the end they could not be retyped fair, but each copy was amended by hand by Farrell, Rennie and other members of the staff sitting round the wardroom table of *Hood*. Now a day's hard work on the forthcoming operation reduced itself to two pages of a long signal pad and went out under its Time of Origin 1730 on the 5th July:

SECRET HAND MESSAGE

To: V.A.A. *Hood Ark Royal Valiant Arethusa Enterprise* D.8 *Fearless Foxhound Forester Escort Wishart Vortigern Vidette Active Versatile* (R) A.C.N.A. 200 Group R.A.F.

From: V. A. FORCE H.

Following orders for Operation Lever. All times Zone (−1).
2. *Dunkerque* believed damaged and aground 35° 44′ N. 00° 42′ W. heading west and most other French ships either sunk or left Oran.
3. French Fleet probably concentrating Toulon. French S/Ms believed at sea. French Air Force probably active in Oran area.
4. Italian Fleet reported off Algiers 4th July. Reliability uncertain.
5. *S/M Proteus* patrolling off Cape Khamis or moving there from Oran.
6. Flying boats from Gibraltar line Cape Palos to Cape Tenez.

7. Intend putting *Dunkerque* out of action for at least one year with gunfire.

8. If gunfire proves impracticable, bombing, mining or torpedo bombing may be used in certain circumstances.

9. After leaving Gibraltar Force H consisting of ships addressed will 'feint' to westward until after dark 5th July and then proceed towards Oran at *Valiant*'s best speed.

10. *Ark Royal*, *Enterprise* and three destroyers will be detached to operate about 80 miles westward of Oran.

11. Remainder of Force H will arrive approximately seven miles North of Oran about 0900 Saturday, 6th July and exercise intention as soon as practicable.

12. Zero hour will be opening fire by *Hood* and *Valiant* and will be 0900 unless otherwise ordered. Other action is to be taken without further orders (except where shown) on the lines of following programme.

13. *Dawn* (a) Air reconnaissance to eastward of *Ark Royal* and of Battle Squadron;
    (b) A/S patrols for *Ark Royal* and Battle Squadron;
    (c) Fighter patrols for Battle Squadron.

14. *Zero—30 minutes Valiant* fly off spotting aircrafting for herself and *Hood* (when ordered). *Dunkerque*'s exact position and ship's head and general situation in Mers-el-Kebir and Oran harbours to be reported.

15. *Zero—15 minutes*
    (a) Relief spotting aircraft from *Ark Royal* escorted by Skuas to be over Oran Bay.
    (b) Skuas dive bombing on forts to be over Oran Bay.

16. *Zero Hour. Hood* and *Valiant* to open fire on *Dunkerque* when ordered.

17. Zero Hour or as soon as forts open fire (whichever is the earlier)
    (a) Skuas to attack 6-inch batteries at Canastel Point and over Mers-el-Kebir.
    (b) *Arethusa* to engage one of above forts according to her position.
    (c) Destroyers engage any forts within range without leaving screen.
    (d) Secondary armaments of capital ships to be reserved for A.A. fire unless essential to engage the forts.
    (e) Destroyers may be ordered to make smoke to cover the Battle Squadron from forts for which they may leave the screen but must not foul line of fire to *Dunkerque*.

189

(*f*) Cruisers and destroyers to shift fire to light craft if attacking.

There, encapsulated in seventeen clauses, lay the blueprint for further disaster and as the day went through and every detail of the action planned for the morrow had to be checked and rechecked, the appalling consequences again impelled Somerville to protest.

After consideration of the proposed operation it became clear that it could only be carried out at the expense of further and considerable loss of French lives and damage to property on shore, owing to the position in which *Dunkerque* was aground. I represented this to Their Lordships in my message 1800/5th July and expressed the view that further loss of French lives would provoke the French to far more active measures against British ships. In view of our already difficult situation in the Western Mediterranean, and since the French dispositions did not indicate any immediate intention to move *Dunkerque*, I asked if any compromise could be reached concerning the demilitarisation of the ship.

This message crossed Admiralty message 1721/5th July directing me to consider the question of giving warning before opening fire, and also the possibility of obtaining French agreement to allow us to destroy *Dunkerque* by demolition, thus saving loss of life.

This incredible suggestion, in view of what they had done on 3rd July, took their breath away and they may well have asked themselves in *Hood* that day whether there was anyone at the Admiralty or in the War Cabinet who could be even dimly aware of the facts of life. Somerville's calm rejoinder is what he wrote in his report of proceedings: what he said at the time is not on record but can be imagined.

In my reply to the Admiralty, 2209/5th July, I expressed the view that it was highly improbable the French at Oran would receive a delegate from Force H, and that to give warning prior to bombardment would be likely to provoke full-scale air and submarine attack on Force H. I suggested, however, that the French authorities might be warned that, unless they took steps to destroy *Dunkerque*, we would reserve the right to do so and the responsibility would be theirs.

Meanwhile Force H (less *Resolution*) had put to sea and were clear of Gibraltar by 2000. After making a feint to the westward till after dark, course was shaped towards Oran and speed increased to 22 and later 23 knots. It is doubtful if the feint of a large force in the Straits achieves its object, since the very bright lights of Ceuta should enable any careful observer to mark the passage of large darkened ships.

His counsel prevailed. The Admiralty changed its collective mind.

At 0250 on the 6th July, I received Admiralty message 0224/6th July cancelling the bombardment of *Dunkerque* and ordering continuous aircraft torpedo attack to be carried out until she was thoroughly damaged.

From wondering if there was anyone at the Admiralty who had a grip on things, they were now somewhat ruefully regretting that there obviously was. All their careful work of the previous day went overboard.

This necessitated a complete reorganisation of the flying programme for bombardment. In spite of this and the time occupied in passing the signal to *Ark Royal* by shaded lamp, she reported she would be ready by 0515.

Meanwhile in Mers-el-Kebir, they had no doubt whatever that the British would be coming back. The *Echo d'Oran* had published an article on 5th July, based on Admiral Estéva's luckless statement, saying that *Dunkerque* had not suffered great damage, that a party of naval constructors had visited the ship and that it would soon be repaired. This caused considerable resentment to the working party on board who had none of them had much sleep since the 3rd July.

In particular, *Enseigne de Vaisseau* Putz knew the article to be a complete fabrication. As part of the Damage Control section, he was aware of what had happened to the ship better than most. He, too, had not had much sleep. He, too, knew that no naval constructors of any note had come aboard and the ship's officers and men had been left very much alone to cope with the situation.

The Admiral and his staff had gone ashore, other Officers and men were accommodated in the *Champoleon* in Oran, and those who remained had been seriously overworked. All were thoroughly exhausted. Tempers were short and rows broke out. All of them now awaited with some considerable misgiving the British attack they were certain would be on its way, only surprised that it had not come on them before.

In London the daily Cabinet meeting on Friday, 5th July, was informed: 'Admiral Somerville was proceeding that afternoon to dispose finally of the ships which had been partially disabled. After that he would proceed to Dakar to deal with the *Richelieu*. They were also informed of a telegram received from the Consul-General, Dakar, stating that the Mayor of Dakar considered that a show of force should be made by the British Fleet, if possible by 10th July, and the Prime Minister said that General Spears was that morning interviewing General de Gaulle with a view to ascertaining whether he (General de Gaulle) was prepared to be put ashore somewhere behind Dakar with a view to rallying French forces in that neighbourhood.

The news from Alexandria was also better. An agreement between the C.-in-C. Mediterranean and Admiral Godfroy had been concluded by which: '(*a*) All oil fuel was to be discharged immediately from French ships; (*b*) The ships would be placed immediately in a condition in which they could not fight; (*c*) The discharge of ships' companies would be a matter for further discussion'.

It was, therefore, only in the Western Mediterranean where matters still remained to be settled. So the interim days came to an end and the next attack began.

'Accordingly at 0520 on 6th July,' Somerville wrote, 'when in position 36° 19′ North 2° 23′ West (that is about ninety miles from Oran) torpedo bomber striking forces were flown off from *Ark Royal* together with Skua aircraft to provide fighter protection and three separate torpedo attacks were carried out on *Dunkerque*. . . .'

Chapter 15

The first squadron of six Swordfish – those antique-looking biplanes for which the Fleet Air Arm at the time had such a quirkish affection – took off at 0520 armed with torpedoes set to run at 27 knots at a depth of 12 feet. It was still dark. A landfall was made at Hababis Island and course was then shaped to keep 15 miles from the coast so as to be in an 'Up Sun' position from the target when the sun rose. No. 820 Squadron was by this time at 7000 feet.

As soon as the first rays of the sun, rising above a thick haze, were seen to strike the *Dunkerque*, the squadron commenced a shallow dive in line ahead down the path of the sun. Aircraft attacked in succession, coming in low over the breakwater. The Squadron was under the command of Lieutenant Commander G. B. Hodgkinson, R.N., who had led the dusk attack on the *Strasbourg* off Oran three days previously.

Complete surprise was achieved and no opposition was encountered except that one of the six aircraft was fired on by a machine-gun during the get away. According to the Squadron Commander, who was the Observer in the leading aircraft, five out of the six torpedoes hit the target. One of these five, however, failed on impact and after running up the ship's side eventually struck a jetty and exploded. The sixth torpedo missed and exploded on the beach at St André. The time was half past six in the morning.

The six Swordfish then returned to *Ark Royal* over a calm sea from which the haze had already begun to lift. This first squadron had gone in on its own without fighter protection. Twenty minutes later three more torpedo-carrying Swordfish from No. 810 Squadron made a further attack under the command of Captain A. C. Newsom, R.M. This half squadron had taken off an hour previously in 7/10th low cloud lying at 500 to 1000 feet and at the same time six Skuas were flown off as fighter protection. They were to be needed.

Unfortunately for the British, the low protective cloud ceased about six miles from the objective. The sub-flight formed up in line astern at 2000 feet close to the shore coast of Oran in order to come on the target from up sun. They turned to attack at 0647 and from then on came under heavy anti-aircraft fire. Violent avoiding action was taken during the approach. The attack was delivered over the shattered breakwater and they thus had an ideal, stationary target beam on to their approach.

Captain Newsom in aircraft 2A attacked first. As he passed over the breakwater, his air gunner saw some men running to man a gun, gave them a burst of fire with his rear gun and dispersed them. The pilot, alas, had omitted to turn on his master switch and thus failed to drop his torpedo. The second aircraft, 2G, attacked next. That torpedo was seen to hit by the pilot of the third and last aircraft, 4F, whose torpedo also struck home.

As the sub-flight was making its getaway, a large explosion was observed in the direction of the *Dunkerque* which by this time was out of sight behind the headland of Fort Santon. The 6-inch and 4-inch batteries from the east of Oran to Mers-el-Kebir point kept up a continuous and accurate anti-aircraft fire until the sub-flight had reformed well out to sea. All bursts were black and many burst within 20 yards of the aircraft. The sound of the burst could be distinctly heard and the concussion felt by the aircraft. No casualties were sustained but a bullet passed through the main spar of the port lower main plane of 4F, the last aircraft to attack. This, however, did not affect the airworthiness of the aircraft.

By the time the second sub-flight of No. 810 Squadron flew off from *Ark Royal* to make the final torpedo attack, the French were fully alert and able to mount considerable opposition. This group of three Swordfish, under the command of Lieutenant

D. F. Godfrey Faussett, R.N., had by far the toughest time. This final attack was made from the opposite direction to the others. The visibility was still hazy and there were patches of low cloud at 1500 feet. Landfall was made ten minutes before seven a.m. and they passed over Cap Falcon at 4000 feet. But there was no protective cloud over the headland. Immediately they came within range, the *Provence* with her quarterdeck awash, the *Mogador* and the shore batteries opened up a heavy barrage of anti-aircraft fire.

Weaving violently to avoid this peppering, they made their final approach low over St André town. The first aircraft, piloted by Lieutenant Godfrey Faussett, dropped its torpedo at short range. This torpedo struck the *Dunkerque* amidships on the port side. A large swirl was observed but no one could be certain whether the torpedo exploded.

The second aircraft, piloted by Sub-Lieutenant R. B. Pearson, R.N., dropped its torpedo at a longer range. Unfortunately a tug about a hundred yards from the *Dunkerque* was in the direct line of fire. The tug, as the pilot curtly observed, disintegrated. The third aircraft dropped its torpedo at short range. This hit the *Dunkerque* but failed to explode.

By now the six Skua aircraft from No. 803 Squadron giving fighter protection to the 'stringbags' were having continuous dog fights with Curtiss Hawk, Morane and Dewoitine fighters bearing French military markings. These aircraft had considerably better performance capabilities than the Skuas. Yet there were no casualties in men or aircraft.

Lieutenant J. M. Christian, R.N., who was in command of this squadron, said that: 'although vastly outmanœuvred by the French aircraft, the French pilots did not seem to care to press home their attacks and in many cases our pilots found themselves in such positions that would certainly have resulted in damage had the French pilots fired seriously. Dog fights lasted for over half an hour, during which time all the Swordfish escaped. Blue Leader [that was himself in command of the squadron] remained for a further forty minutes on patrol, but beyond A.A. fire was not attacked again. All our aircraft returned independently, Blue three having been literally escorted out to sea for half an hour by seven French fighters.'

Individual pilots reported to similar effect. 'Curtiss Hawk aircraft appeared to be working in pairs. Lower one providing sitting target until attacked, when it quickly outmanœuvred Skua, one in rear and above diving down on to Skua's tail.' As a result of this combat: 'Own port guns put out of action. Holes in tail plane and holes and large rent in starboard main plane, large rent in fuselage, but attacking aircraft broke off into cloud.'

Another report read:

The Dewoitine retired losing height with smoke coming from engine after a dog fight lasting about 30 minutes. Own aircraft spun three times. The French did not appear to put their heart into the fight. If they had done so, their superior performance would have told on the Skuas.

Enemy did not fire or fired very wide. He was always in position after avoiding action and could not be got in sights. If enemy had been trying, he could not have helped shooting Skua down. Rear gunner unable to fire owing to avoiding action.

Enemy stall turned and dived steeply seawards through cloud.

Attacked one of the flights of three Moranes. They were joined by a further four aircraft and we fought rearguard action until reaching safety of layer of clouds. No hits were observed. The French fighters appeared to be holding their fire.

Enemy in every case appeared to be unwilling to engage our aircraft closely. Many situations arose where, due to vastly superior performance, the enemy could have inflicted casualties, but resisted doing so.

The most dramatic of these combats was that carried out by Sub-Lieutenant (A) R. B. Pearson, R.N., in Fairey Swordfish No. A2C of No. 810 Squadron, one of the final torpedo attackers on *Dunkerque*. 'This was a very stout effort', his Admiral wrote, 'to evade the attack of four Dewoitine fighters successfully *and* to engage them in return with a Swordfish.'

This is put into context by a recital of the damage the 'stringbag' sustained and yet got back to the carrier.

A shell passed through the fuselage cowling on the port side of the rear cockpit in line with the rear gun and burst on the starboard upper aileron. Scarf ring bent. One Lewis gun magazine damaged. Bullet through the W/T transmitter. Bullet through spare coil. Spare Lewis gun piston rod bent. Port upper longeron bent. Both port elevator wires partially severed. Tail actuating gear control cables severed. Several ribs in starboard lower main plane damaged. Centre section rear main spar damaged.

It was in the tradition of World War I that this ancient biplane yet managed to fight her way back to *Ark Royal* in a more or less airworthy condition.

Whilst making a getaway from a torpedo attack on the French battlecruiser and at a height of about 100 feet some small splashes were seen on the port bow. Although no fighters were seen, it was realised that the splashes were caused by machine-gun fire from above. The observer reported that he saw a fighter turning away. A few seconds later the observer reported that there was a fighter approaching from the direction of the sun on the starboard quarter.

The pilot immediately turned steeply to starboard and noticed a large burst of machine-gun fire in the water on the port bow. A third attack was made exactly the same as the others and the rounds missed to port as before. It was not until the fighter broke away after this attack that the pilot of A2C saw him for the first time.

The fighter turned back and attacked from astern. The pilot of A2C turned 180° and dived beneath the fighter. It was in this attack that the pilot of A2C thinks that most of the hits on his aircraft occurred. The fighter gave up the attack, but was followed by another of the same type. The same tactics were employed as before and the pilot was able to turn beneath him and fire about 50 rounds with his front gun.

The fighter made off at great speed and A2C was unable to follow. The rear gunner managed to fire a few bursts at the first fighter but the violent manœuvring and damage to his scarf ring made it impossible to fire accurately.

So the attack ended and the British flew back to their aircraft carrier, having executed with professional skill and great private disgust the task they had been ordered to do. What of the *Dunkerque*, the target they had been directed to put out of action for at least a year?

The great ship was now an appalling sight. Already aground,

the additional damage done to her now put out of question any possibility of her getting away to sea as a fighting vessel in foreseeable time. In the words of *Enseigne de Vaisseau* Putz the scene was '*hallucinante*' – a word perhaps best translated in this context by the two words 'catastrophic' and 'haunting'.

The reasons for this were complex, but principal amongst them was the fact that the previous evening a large auxiliary vessel, the trawler *Terre Neuve*, had moored alongside the *Dunkerque* in order to evacuate the remaining personnel from the ship the following day.

Putz, who had had very little rest in the last sixty hours, had installed himself in a cabin opposite the wardroom just abaft the '*pont château*' – the upperworks which ran forward from that point. During the late evening of the 5th when the *Terre Neuve* had come alongside up forward on the starboard side he had gone out on deck to take a look at her. He had last seen the *Terre Neuve* some months previously when on patrol north of Scandinavia in the Barents Sea. As he stood looking at her, he found '*le grand Pierre*', Commander Tanguy, standing beside him also gazing down on the '*chalutier*'.

The *Terre Neuve* was an ocean-going trawler adapted for war purposes by the addition of anti-submarine depth charge rails on which there now stood the full complement of those deadly cylindrical barrels of T.N.T. ready to roll off in quick succession once a lurking submarine had been detected. In the centre of these barrels a tubular detonator was placed, set to work at different depths. Naturally now that the vessel was in harbour and in use as a transport, the detonators had been removed so that the depth charges were nominally safe. This was certainly all right in so far as normal harbour or ship accidents were concerned.

'They'd make a good firework display if ever they did go up,' Tanguy said almost to himself, a remark which later proved to be tragically prophetic.

That same Friday evening, two days after the first British attack, they had been warned in the *Dunkerque* that the British were coming back, probably the next day, to finish off the ship.

The C.-in-C. had ordered the remaining personnel on board to evacuate the ship, for the A.A. guns not to be manned and for anti-aircraft protection to be afforded by the coastal batteries. There were then only some 380 officers and men left aboard. These had all been ceaselessly employed since the débâcle in clearing up the mess and in making preparations for the *Dunkerque* to repair herself as best she could so that later on she could be got away to a dockyard where she could be fully restored.

When the British attacked at dawn, Putz was asleep. The alert began to be sounded over the loudspeakers blaring at everyone urgently to evacuate the ship at the utmost speed by means of the *Terre Neuve* and other boats alongside. But it was already too late. Putz dressed as quickly as he could and was just pulling on his seaboots when he heard a number of explosions on the starboard side. He ran out on deck and went forward.

A scene of almost indescribable confusion met his eyes, already accustomed as they had been over the last two days to sights and experiences he would never forget for the rest of his life. This was the first attack and up forward, by the two great gun turrets, a mass of twisted and jagged metal lay strewn about the deck like some monstrous junkyard. Men were buried under this mass of steel, some of them dead, some of them terribly wounded. The living, the dying and the newly dead were all inextricably mingled with the coffins and corpses which yet remained from the previous assault on the ship.

Even disciplined men panic when the terror they have to face is too great to endure. Putz saw his friend Bonafos de la Tour, another *Enseigne de Vaisseau*, leap from the considerable height of the upper deck into the water already newly strewn with wreckage. Men were crying out for help, some without arms or legs, some who would soon be mercifully dead. Men were crowding down on to the after deck of the *Terre Neuve*. To begin with Putz got caught up in the rush; then, remembering his responsibilities as an officer, he went back on board the *Dunkerque* to let the others get away first.

Everything appeared to be out of control for the moment. There were not enough stretchers – how could there be? Hammocks and tarpaulins were pressed into service – anything which could somehow or other carry a man – and these were dragged bumping along the deck with their pathetic loads by those who had not been wounded. It was a nightmare.

Just before the second attack took place, Putz was helping to carry towards the *Terre Neuve* a Quartermaster whose thigh had been broken. He was a heavy man in an agony of pain and as they were dragging him as best they could along the deck, his shattered thigh banging on every obstruction, the guns opened up on the next aircraft coming in to the attack. The regular Pim-Pam Pim-Pam of the 70-mm anti-aircraft guns beat a grotesque accompaniment to the half-dead man's progress along the deck and when they reached the ship's side they were forced almost literally to throw him down on to the deck of the *Terre Neuve* and then run for cover as the aircraft tore in to the attack.

It was then that the worst disaster of all in human terms took place. Putz and his party had taken shelter near a hatch under the armoured deck when one of the torpedoes from this second attack struck the *Terre Neuve* itself and set off the depth charges on the stern as if their own detonators had been in place. This was the greatest explosion he had heard in his life. A few moments after it was over, they came out on deck into what at first sight appeared to be a dense black rain. The explosion had sent up a vast column of water, coal, steel and wreckage of every kind hundreds of feet in the air and this was coming down like a deluge. In such a disaster one's sense of time changes and Putz thought it would never end as he peered out, dazed and stunned, through the murk.

Then followed a complete and absolute silence. Not a sound could be heard. There were no groans nor crying from the stricken. There was no movement but for the falling débris, simply a terrible awe-inspiring stillness, as if the end of the world had come.

Then gradually life began again and the extent of the catastrophe became apparent to those who were left alive. The *Terre Neuve* had sunk and the *Dunkerque* herself was settling deeper into the water. A complete evacuation of everyone left on board was ordered. The aftermath had begun.

Chapter 16

That evening of Saturday, 6th July 1940, saw Force H back in Gibraltar and Admiral Gensoul take an aeroplane to Toulon, 'where what was left of my Fleet was to be found and where I hoisted my flag in the *Strasbourg*'. The *Commandant Teste* had already sailed for Bizerta. Only the crippled destroyer *Mogador*, the half-sunk battleship *Provence* and the totally disabled *Dunkerque* remained in the desolation of Mers-el-Kebir.

'And so that filthy job is over at last', Somerville wrote to his wife. The self-respect, the proper satisfaction and the shining image which every naval officer who aspires to command a Fleet at sea carries in his mind of the honourable conduct and bearing of the Royal Navy had been loathsomely tarnished. Done counter to their instinct, to their advice (which it took guts to proffer) and to their deep feelings of comradeship, it was an offence against the spirit.

'It all seemed so rosy,' Somerville went on to his wife about his appointment as Commander-in-Chief, 'and it's all been so horrible.' Legitimate pride in one's achievement – not arrogance, not vainglory – is essential to every man in the work to which he devotes his life, and where was pride after Mers-el-Kebir?

'If there is a stain on the flag,' Admiral Gensoul had said as he buried his dead in the cemetery of Oran, 'it is certainly not on ours.' 47 French officers, 196 Petty Officers and 1054 ratings had been killed. A further 351 had been wounded. It was a gruesome butcher's bill.

'The distress of the British Admiral and his principal officers was evident to us from the signals which had passed,' Churchill wrote later. 'Nothing but the most direct orders compelled them to open fire on those who had been so lately their comrades.'

'Afraid I shall get a colossal raspberry from the Admiralty,' Somerville went on to his wife, 'for letting the battlecruiser escape. In fact I shouldn't be surprised if I was relieved forthwith. I don't mind because it was an absolutely bloody business to shoot up those Frenchmen who showed the greatest gallantry. The truth is my heart wasn't in it and you're not allowed a heart in wartime . . . we all feel thoroughly dirty and ashamed that the first time we should have been in action was an affair like this . . . but, as I warned the Admiralty, I think it was the biggest political blunder of modern times and I imagine will rouse the whole world against us. . . .'

It certainly did. The German reaction was predictable. 'The German Press has exploded in anger,' *The Times* reported, 'at what flaring headlines in the evening newspapers describe as a "cowardly British attack on the French Fleet".' The *Berliner Nachtausgabe* called it 'the greatest act of scoundrelism in world history'. The *Berliner Beersen Zeitung*, often used as the mouthpiece of the German High Command was reported in *The Times* as having said:

Germany had given a binding undertaking that the Reich had no intention of seizing the French naval fleet. Churchill ignores this incontestable act and summoning every element of brutality at his disposal, orders an attack on French ships. With unique but pitiable notoriety, this hero of unparalleled ignominy, Churchill, achieves the distinction of being the greatest criminal in the world. We are anxious to see whether there is still enough sense of honour left in the British people to make them separate themselves now from a Prime Minister who stands in the pillory of world condemnation. Have the British people not courage enough to free themselves from this crime and from the one who is responsible for it? If not the English people will themselves be treated as criminals.

'It has been a bitter road from the glorious co-operation of our two navies at Dunkirk to the melancholy action at Oran,' A. V. Alexander, the First Lord of the Admiralty, said in Parliament. 'Nothing would have rejoiced us so much as to continue in comradeship till the final victory but we used all the persuasion and tried every solution which could be expected of us without incurring risks which might well have been dangerous to our cause. Nevertheless, there must be no recriminations.'

Well, yes . . . it is easy to be wise in 1972 about events in 1940, the facts of which have been truly established. But the complex values which make up the climate of the day have also to be borne in mind. The intellectual analysis is always only a part of the picture. How did people feel at the time?

So far as the French Navy was concerned, there was very naturally a complete loathing and disgust best expressed by the words, '*Les salauds!*' A few days later the officers of the *Dunkerque*, who had established their mess in the villa of a local business man in Oran, sent back to Admiral Somerville the various gifts and souvenirs they had received from British ships and in particular their 'chummy ship' HMS *Hood*.

Accompanying these trophies was a sad little note signed by all the officers present. '*Le Commandant et les Officiers du* Dunkerque *vous font part de la mort, pour l'honneur de leur pavillon, les 3 et 6 juillet* 1940 *de neuf officiers et de* 200 *hommes de leur bâtiment. Ils vous retournent les souvenirs ci-joints qu'ils tenaient de leurs camarades de combat de la Marine Royale britannique, en qui ils avaient placé toute leur confiance. Et ils vous expriment à cette occasion toute leur amère tristesse et leur dégoût de voir que ces camarades n'ont pas hésité à souiller le glorieux pavillon de St Georges d'une tâche ineffaçable, celle d'un assassinat*'. . . . 'The Captain and Officers of the *Dunkerque* inform you of the death for the honour of their flag on the 3rd and 6th July 1940 of nine officers and 200 men of their ship. They return to you herewith the souvenirs they had of their comrades in arms of the Royal Navy in whom they had placed all their trust. And they express to you on this occasion all their bitter sadness and their disgust at seeing these comrades having no hesitation in soiling the glorious flag of St George with an ineffaceable stain – that of an assassin.'

For General de Gaulle and his newly formed Free French movement, Mers-el-Kebir proved all but lethal. It was 'a terrible blow to our hopes', he said, and the way in which it had been done, in particular the calculated omission to consult him first, greatly increased the friction which was already latent in his wartime relationship with Churchill and the British Government and which was to continue throughout the rest of his life.

In France herself, still numbed by the shock of defeat; with the country slashed into two zones, one under direct German occupation and the other nominally free; with a million and a half of her men prisoners of war; with communications disrupted and a population dazed beyond measure by what had happened to them in the last two months: the outrage of Mers-el-Kebir passed as just one further calamity to which the only reaction was that it was incomprehensible.

They had all been through too much. But as the effect of what had been done sank in, the only real justification for the attack – the fact that the British did not trust Hitler or Mussolini whatever words of honour the great dictators might offer as a token of good faith – this passed unnoticed and the ancient cry went up that England was again 'the hereditary enemy'.

For Goebbels and the German propaganda machine, Mers-el-Kebir was a gift. At his daily conference held at the Ministry of Propaganda on 4th July 1940, Goebbels said:

The British Navy's attack on the French Fleet at Oran is to be used for a detailed exposition of how Britain first dragged France into the war, how she then let France make the main preparations, how France was required to supply most of the materials, how the struggle was fought on French soil, how French divisions bled themselves white while the British carried out a 'withdrawal without losses' policy, how Britain eventually tried to force the French to continue the struggle, how the British abused them after the collapse and blamed them for the defeat, how they then set up a French pseudo-government on British soil and how, to top it all, they were now attacking the French ships – all 'in France's interest'. Here Britain has really revealed herself without her mask.

Posters appeared in Paris depicting a French sailor, his wife and new-born baby standing with tragic expressions on their faces amidst the ruins, menaced by a brutal British officer and with captions such as 'Remember Oran!' 'Thus ends the *Entente Cordiale!*' 'The English did this!'

This propaganda had the double object of destroying any French respect or love for England and replacing it with hatred, while at the same time distracting attention from the highly unpopular curfew which the occupation forces had just imposed. But Goebbels, as always, overdid and backed up this smear campaign with another poster showing a smiling young German soldier holding in his arms a boy happily munching a biscuit. This went out with the caption, 'Abandoned people trust the German soldier!' It was a nice idea but the graffiti added by Parisians soon made this piece of propaganda somewhat counter-productive.

However, it was Darlan on whom the effect was most telling. The Fleet was virtually his own creation, he was completely identified with its fate and he took the attack personally. Described by one historian as 'Drunk with anguish and rage, his entire being was directed at that time to ideas of revenge'. Blind anger made him take the extraordinary decision, without consulting anyone, to suggest to the Italian Admiralty that they should take over the *Strasbourg* and together attack the British Fleet at Alexandria with a view to liberating Admiral Godfroy.

This was a highly dangerous move. Marshal Badoglio at once seized the opportunity of asking France to put her North African bombers at his disposal in order to attack the British Fleet. But by this time Darlan had consulted with Laval, Baudouin and the venerable Marshal Pétain, who was appalled at the suggestion of joining up with the Italians. A firm and final 'No' was handed down to the Admiral of the Fleet, who had to content himself with the half-hearted reprisal raid on Gibraltar. As a footnote to this, however, it has to be remembered that between June 1940 and the Italian surrender in September 1943, two cruisers, ten destroyers, seven submarines, six corvettes and eight minesweepers were transferred by the Vichy Government to Italy and manned by Italian crews.

There were repercussions, too, from the senior British naval officers concerned with the operation. Captain Holland was so deeply distressed that he asked to be relieved of his command of *Ark Royal* and thus virtually ended any ambition he may have had for his Flag. Admiral North at Gibraltar also insisted on being heard. He wrote to the Admiralty that: 'he felt it might be of value to place on record the views which had prevailed in the Mediterranean in the light of our knowledge of the situation'.

Many an Admiral has taken on Their Lordships – or the Establishment, if you like – and none has ever come out on top. Even Nelson could not ensure the one thing he cared about at the end of his life – the future security of his beloved Emma Hamilton. Admiral North was to be no exception to this extraordinary rule that Authority, like the Deity, can do no wrong. It seems to us now that it can and does all the time, but in 1940 on 17th July Their Lordships replied to this recalcitrant Admiral that:

The opinions of Senior Officers are always of value before an operation is carried out: but once the operation has taken place Their Lordships strongly deprecate comments on a policy which has been decided by the Admiralty in the light of factors which were either known or unknown to officers on the spot.

In this case Their Lordships were never under the delusion that the French Fleet would not fight in the last instance and this fact was taken fully into consideration in the preliminary deliberations.

The contents . . . of your letter show a most dangerous lack of appreciation of the manner in which it is intended to conduct the war.

Their Lordships fully realised how repugnant the operation would be to all officers concerned but they cannot allow such considerations to influence decisions in war and are surprised that comment of the kind received should have been made.

Admiral North was later to pay very dearly for the gesture he had made.

Perhaps, though, it is Admiral Gensoul who suffered at the hands of the French Establishment of the day the worst indignity it could then apply. He was to be totally ignored.

He left a sad record of his treatment:

I wrote my report of proceedings on the 9th July and I cannot remember how exactly I got it to Vichy. Admiral Darlan came to Toulon on the 19th July and asked me no questions whatever on Mers-el-Kebir. I tried to talk to him without success but he never said a word. He was clearly giving me the cold shoulder but he never reproached me. Vichy never asked me for any clarification of the tragedy of Mers-el-Kebir.

As I was on the upper age limit, I was appointed on the 8th August Inspector of Maritime Forces, a purely honorary function, but which gave me my five stars (full Admiral) and put back my retiring age by two years.

On the 10th August I disembarked from the *Strasbourg*.

On the 16th August I was summoned to Vichy by the Admiralty where I was received by Admirals Darlan and Le Luc. They said I needed a rest and should take a few days off from my new appointment as Inspector of Maritime Forces. They did not say one word to me about Mers-el-Kebir.

On the 18th August I lunched with Admiral Darlan at his home on the outskirts of Vichy. Also present were General and Madame Weygand as well as Borotra. The question of Mers-el-Kebir was scarcely mentioned. I then took up my appointment at Vichy where I remained until September 1942, when I was placed on the Retired List. I never said one word to Laval. I only saw Marshal Pétain long afterwards when he visited the Exhibition of Marine Works: neither then nor in the course of other very rare interviews I had with him, was there ever any question of Mers-el-Kebir. I never saw Baudouin . . . I was never criticised for compressing the terms of the British ultimatum [i.e. for omitting the vital alternative of sailing the Fleet to the West Indies]. No one ever talked to me about it. I was definitely kept at arm's length without ever knowing why.

Time moved on. The great sweep of action in that extraordinary summer of 1940 took the war elsewhere. Force H duly went to Dakar to deal with the *Richelieu* and in England the crucial Battle of Britain began. In spite of German propaganda, in spite of Darlan's feelings and the ambivalent attitude of the Vichy Government, the memory of Mers-el-Kebir became submerged in the torrent of daily events. What had been done was not forgotten, it was simply and for a time overlaid.

Until Hitler turned east into Russia in the summer of the following year – perhaps until America entered the war after Pearl Harbour in December 1941, the struggle, titanic in scale though it was, remained simple and clear. Germany had overrun Europe except for that pocket torch of an island, the United Kingdom, where one man's valour turned the pocket torch into a blazing beacon of light.

It is a truism yet nevertheless an inescapable fact that, but for Churchill, the world of today would certainly be a very different place. At that time England stood quite alone and Churchill, at the pinnacle of his power, kept the fighting spirit of freedom alive. The rest of us followed on. It is sentimental and perhaps naïve to say that Churchill's leadership alone was the chief generative factor in the winning of the war. He was a man, and men make terrible mistakes. Without him, though, from the fall of France until the entry of the United States, what would have happened to the world we know? We can all of us make a fairly plausible guess.

So what is the verdict now? A number of books have been written on Mers-el-Kebir, and when I set out to research and to write this one, I said to the many people who so kindly and warmly helped me with their experiences and the facts I needed, that it was neither my purpose nor my function to sit in judgment on the events and the reasons why. The reader can do this for himself.

The tragedy that took place was consummate and perhaps need never have happened at all. Perhaps. . . . Certainly there will never be agreement and certainly it is those who suffered most who have the right, possibly the only right to decide on the values.

For me it is certainly true that all civilised men have two countries and one of them is France. I love France and I respect and admire the French. Now that I have spent the better part of a year immersed in the horror with which this book deals, I find myself deeply moved by this tiny example of how little man's destiny seems to lie within his own control. We achieve the extraordinary feat of going to the moon and, as I write, we have the obscenities of Belfast. The paradox of life is so often agonising, so often incomprehensible, so often meaningless even to the most bigoted doctrinaire who cushions his spirit with deeply embedded prejudice. What is it all about? And in the case of Mers-el-Kebir why *did* it happen?

When I began my researches, one of the principal characters who took part in that dreadful day of 3rd July said to me: 'Why write the book at all? Why bring it up all over again?' He was an Englishman and the British certainly have no pride in what happened at Mers-el-Kebir. But was it necessity or wasn't it? Was Churchill right or wrong?

I had no proper answer to give him at the time and, indeed, for a while wondered if perhaps he might not be right and I should abandon the book. But now it is done, I think perhaps I know why. I may not have succeeded in re-creating in all its dire tragedy those grim hours in the first year of the war when for the first time in a hundred and twenty-five years the British fired on the French. It is difficult in 1972 to bring alive the world as it was in 1940 especially to those who were not even born at that time.

But this book does not set out to judge, nor to argue who was right or who was wrong. In any case what does it matter? There is no going back to put things right – in the way a Communist will rewrite history every time the party line changes – what is done is done and the facts are there. But at least we can try to understand, the smallest tribute we can pay to those who suffered and those who died. Has this not been the purpose of tragedy since the times of the Greeks?

Part of the agony of Mers-el-Kebir was caused by faulty or inadequate communication. Nothing really got through until it was all too late. At least here – in our ability to communicate – there does seem, thirty years after the Second World War, a growing point, however small, in the human condition. To link communication with understanding is perhaps one of things it is all about. . . .

Bibliography

La Marine Française pendant la Seconde Guerre Mondiale, Amiral Auphan and Jacques Mordal, Hachette, 1958.

Mers-el-Kebir, Pierre Varillon, Amiot-Dumont, 1949.

Mers-el-Kebir, Denis Baldensperger, Rouf, 1967.

Nouveaux Grands Dossiers de l'histoire contemporaine, Robert Aron, Perrin, 1964.

Fighting Admiral, Donald MacIntyre, Evans, 1961.

The Fleet that faced both ways, A. Heckstall-Smith, Blond, 1963.

60 Days that Shook the West, J. Benoist-Méchin, Cape, 1963.

Assignment to Catastrophe, Edward Spears, Eyre & Spottiswood.

The Secret Conferences of Dr Goebbels, Willi A. Boelke, Weidenfeld & Nicolson, 1966.

The Second World War, Winston S. Churchill, Cassell.

List of French Dead and Wounded classified by rank

	Killed or lost	Wounded
Officers	47	14
Maîtres-principaux	3	—
Premiers-maîtres	16	5
Maîtres	44	11
Seconds-maîtres	134	20
Quartiers-maîtres	352	109
Matelots	701	192
	1,297	351

Index

217

Lyons, 45

Maginot line, 29, 30, 78, 103
Maintenon, 50
Malta, G.C., 59
Mandel, Georges, 43, 53, 54
Margesson, Capt. David, 15
Marseilles, 45, 124, 125, 177
Martinique, 13, 70, 145, 149
Massiglia, French ship, 43, 53
Mers-el-Kebir, 23-6, 29, 35-6, 52-3, 60-4, 66, 70, 72-6, 79-80, 82-4,
    88-9, 92-3, 100, 103, 110, 113, 118-19, 123, 125-37, 146, 150-60,
    164-8, 172-9, 181, 185, 187, 191, 194, 202, 204-5, 208-10
Michelier, Vice-Admiral, 134, 162, 163, 182-3
Mittelhauser, General, 43, 51
Mogador, French ship, 136, 152, 159, 161, 174, 195, 202
Monnet, Jean, 15, 35
Moreau, Admiral, 27
Morice, Deputy Governor, 54
Morton, Desmond, 131-2
Mussolini, Benito, 34, 35, 39, 110, 205

Narvik, 156
Négadelle, *Capitaine*, 92, 123
Nelson, H.M.S., 154
Nelson, Lord, 207
Nérac, 66, 88, 91, 97, 123, 124, 133, 146
Newsom, Capt. A. C., R.N., 194
Noguès, General, 16, 53
Normandie class ships, 154
North, Vice-Adm. Sir Dudley, 21, 28, 51-70, 76, 84, 92, 97, 107, 140,
    186, 207

Odend'hal, Admiral, 46
Ollive, Admiral, 26, 107, 141
Oran, 13, 16, 17, 22-6, 51, 53, 60, 63, 69, 70, 72, 74, 75, 78, 80-4, 91,
    99, 100, 107, 117, 122-6, 129, 135, 140, 146, 148, 150-1, 164, 167-
    70, 176, 180-2, 184-6, 190-4, 203, 206
Owensmith, Sub-Lieut., R.N., 135

Pandora, H.M.S., 22, 169, 186
Paris, 33, 35, 45, 50
Pearl Harbor, 209
Pearson, Sub-Lieut. R. B., R.N., 195-6